MONEY BONDAGE

DISCOVER THE POWER OF MIND OVER MONEY

SOPHIE BENNETT

Money Bondage
Discover the power of mind over money

Published by
The Wealth Network Ltd.
P O Box28
Newent
GL18 1WG.
United Kingdom
www.the-wealth-network.com/publishing

Author photograph provided
by John Cleary

Editing, cover design, and interior formatting provided
by Jera Publishing

ISBN: 978-0-9926128-0-1

To Fiona.
Your energy and love lifted the lives of so many - including mine.

Contents

The Pack of Bacon

"Learn from the mistakes of others. You can't live long enough to make them all yourself."
—Eleanor Roosevelt

It all kicked off over a sandwich.

A bacon sandwich to be precise.

I'll never forget that dreadful day. It was a grey day in November, a drab Sunday morning. I was with my partner in our cosy little rented flat, I say cosy because it was about the size of a postage stamp. I had to climb over our few possessions to make it across the living room to get to the kitchen. I was having a rare day off, and my partner and I were both ready for something to eat. I fancied a bacon sandwich.

Oops. I couldn't find any bacon in the fridge, so off to the shops it was; at least that was the idea. Out came his wallet and my purse, and for a few short minutes it was a bit of a joke that we had no cash between us. We were used to it. Things had been a bit tight for quite a while. Except this time, we really didn't have any money. Not a bean.

A few beans would have been a start, but we didn't have any of those either. We would have taken beans gladly that morning. So, there we were, poking around the fridge to see if there was anything to eat that wasn't either mouldy or out of date. Nada.

I started to imagine the smell and the taste of a salty, crispy bacon sandwich. The more I knew I couldn't have it, the more my stomach started to rumble. I was seriously hungry. It was food cruelty, and it wasn't funny.

We looked at each other and realised something. Not only had we both run out of cash, but neither of us had any money in the bank either. Then it really started to sink in; not only were we unable to use our debit cards at an ATM, but we had both maxed out all of our credit cards too. That meant that the last resort of waltzing down to the supermarket and paying with plastic was out of the window as well.

We started to get increasingly agitated. It started a panic. For you to get the full picture, you need to know that I had a very physical job at the time, so when I got hungry, I got really hungry, and when I got hungry, I got cranky. I was getting more cranky by the minute. So we started the hidden money search. You know the one, the search of pockets, bottoms of handbags, scrabbles through kitchen drawers and, as the ultimate last resort, the dig for coins down the back of the sofa.

We combed every inch of that tiny little flat. Then we moved outside. We searched both cars (we were still under the illusion we could afford one car each at that point). We squeezed our hands down into those little awkward gaps around the sides of the seats. We even looked under the floor mats. What was the total of our cash reserves from that almighty search?

The grand sum of 17 pence.

Holy crap. That was it. Our total net worth.

In fact the reality was worse, much worse. Our entire joint true net worth was minus £60,000, give or take a few thousand. You see, we were in debt—big time.

There was no bacon sandwich for us that day. We ended up chomping toast with the leftover bread and finished the few rather dodgy bits of cheese that were lurking at the back of the fridge. We didn't think we could sink much lower.

It seemed impossible that we couldn't even afford a pack of unsmoked Danish. We still refer to it as our "pack of bacon day".

That was the first day that we had to really face up to facts. We were broke, and it couldn't go on.

It wasn't quite the bottom of the pit though; that came the next morning when the repo man turned up to repossess our BMW.

What a nice way to start the week. Something had to be done, and what I discovered on my journey back to solvency (and beyond) is the basis of this book.

If you are having financial challenges yourself, you have many steps to take. The most important step is always the first one, because no journey starts until you take it. When you take that first step, keep asking the right questions and keep on taking small steps; you will be amazed at how far you can travel.

Is Cash-flow Cramping Your Style?

"There are three types of people in this world: those who make things happen, those who watch things happen, and those who wonder what happened."
—Mary Kay Ash

How do you go from being broke to being financially free?

Is it about being in the right place at the right time? Is it luck? Is it hard work? Is it even possible for an ordinary person?

I was financially crippled when I was sitting in my flat that day, hungry and hacked off. It took a little time, but slowly I did start to get on the right track. At first I thought that I had had a few 'lucky' breaks. But I had a problem with that. I didn't want to rely on luck. So I decided to find out; can 'luck' be repeated? Can it be created? Had I been lucky, or had I made my own?

I knew that if I was going to get where I wanted to be in life I had to find out. I couldn't leave the next ten years to chance. When I uncovered the answers I realised that they needed to be shared so that other women could benefit. The seeds for this book were sown.

What I discovered was that I had made my own luck. I also realised that anyone can make their own luck, when they know how to.

If the same types of questions intrigue you, here are a couple of good ones you can ask yourself to get started.

If you were 100% sure that you were NEVER going to win the lottery, would you take your financial planning more seriously?

Here is another useful question. If it was certain that you would never have money that you hadn't earned or received as interest on your investments, would you manage your money differently from day to day?

It's worth making a note of your answers because you will probably want to come back to them later. Here's the best question of all: if you could wave a magic wand and be able guarantee that you couldn't possibly fail in any money making venture at all, what business would you choose?

These are great questions because the reality is this: you probably will never win the lottery, so you might as well start thinking about different ways of getting the money you want. Save your ticket money for something more useful. For a moment, just get the lottery fantasy out of your head. If you don't, just having it as a possibility will hold you back, but more of that later.

I was over 30 before I started to take my future wealth seriously. I had already been in the workforce for more than fifteen years. I had worked crazy hours for all of that time, mostly slaving away seven days a week. I had been going through a painful process of *getting ready*, even though I didn't realise that at the time.

Working all the hours I could find had not helped. I was massively in debt. I had no short-term certainty; I could barely think about the following week without making myself feel sick with worry. I hadn't even dared to consider my long-term financial future up to that point. I didn't own any property. Not only was I broke, I was deeply unhappy about it.

Fast forward to today. Using the ideas and strategies contained in this book, I am a wealthy woman. I am blessed to not need a mortgage. I own more than one house outright. I can afford holidays, horses, hobbies and I enjoy driving a decent car. All those things have been paid for in cash, no credit cards required.

I am a good deal happier too. But *how* I am happier is less about the money than you might think. I will reveal some of the keys to being happier throughout this book, because I have learned how money and happiness are linked—and how they aren't linked. The difference is important for your own happiness. After all, isn't that why you want more money; so you can be happier?

I still work, but now it is only out of choice. I love my work, that's why I keep doing it; however, it has to fit around other important aspects of my life. It's not the only thing I love doing! I got to that point because I learned how to start asking the right questions.

I am no longer a slave to money. I wrote this book because I want as many people as possible to realise that it's possible for anyone who seriously wants it. That means it's possible for you, if you apply yourself, if you are prepared to take responsibility, if you want it badly enough. I learned that if you have the right skills, you can have almost anything you want. So what skills do *you* need? We will explore that together, and you might be surprised by some of the skills that you do (and don't) need.

This book reveals many secrets of success, and how to look after the money that flows from it. Some of them were revealed to me from books, some from people who have helped me, and some from seminars and other educational experiences. All of them I have actually learned by implementation. The secrets have been integrated in my own life to the point where until I sat and wrote them down, I had forgotten they are secrets at all. I had forgotten that most people don't know most of them, and that's why they struggle.

I certainly don't have every financial solution to every money problem, no one does. If anyone did, we would all be millionaires! There are so many variables, so many different people with varying needs and drivers, and so many emotions involved. Yet there are common problems, similar issues and simple solutions that really are applicable to almost every one of us.

Many thoughts, behaviours and actions that we are programmed to consider to be 'normal' in our western culture are destined to bring difficulty and unhappiness for many women. The good news is this: there are better choices open to you; you just need to know what they are.

I can assure you that it is possible to achieve great things without sacrificing your femininity, without wavering from your commitment to the important relationships in your life, without sacrificing loyalty or love. It is possible to collaborate with others and be successful because of it, rather than in spite of it—regardless of what some people say!

During my research, one woman said to me, "It's interesting to hear about your book, but what I want to know is this: will it **inspire** me?" I kept that thought firmly in my mind while writing. That lady made me realise how much we all need inspiration as well as instruction. This is a book for those of you who want to take your future into your own hands.

If you apply this information to your own life, there are no limits to what you can achieve financially, and the journey to financial freedom is a truly inspirational one.

When you get the money you need and want, you can be a better person for it in more ways than you can imagine. You will make some amazing discoveries about yourself along the way too. All you need to get started is the courage to take the first tiny step towards a new life of financial freedom. Here is the good news: you have taken the first one already. Enjoy the book.

What's Your Starting Point?

"If I were you and I was going there, I wouldn't start from here."
—Anon, old Irish joke

I s there a perfect place to start any journey?

There probably is, but I haven't met anyone yet who actually started there! So if you are starting from a less than perfect position, how do you go about the process of getting financially free?

The first thing to realise is this. Anything **really is** possible for you, no matter how awful your starting point may be. As you have already seen, my starting point was pretty dire.

Remember that I started out £60,000.00 in debt. Others have started from even worse points than that. One chap I know started over three MILLION pounds in the red after a failed business venture. He had people with baseball bats trying to get into his house in the middle of the night. He got out of debt, and a whole lot further than solvent. So you can take hope. There are many others who have started from a much worse place than where you probably are now and still cracked it.

Women like Maria Das Gracas Silva Foster. Maria was raised in a Brazilian shantytown, surrounded by poverty that it is difficult to imagine in Europe. She spent her childhood in Morro do Adeus, an extremely poor shantytown area of Rio de Janeiro. Her mother worked constantly and her father was an alcoholic. She collected cans and waste paper to make extra money. Maria secured an internship with Petrobras, a Brazilian oil giant, she broke through barrier after barrier and over time she worked her way up to be the company's first female Head of Field Engineering. Her work ethic was legendary, and she earned her the nickname Caveirao (the name used locally for the unstoppable armoured vehicles the police used to clean up crime-riddled Brazilian neighbourhoods). She became the company's first female CEO in February 2012. She didn't exactly have the best start. But she did it anyway. Incredible. Maria's story is just one example of achievement, and there are many more to come.

True stories are great to read. They provide us with inspiration—that belief that anything is possible, for any one of us. That is why there are so many amazing stories in this book, and I hope that they inspire you. Knowing about other women who have found the courage to dig deeper than they ever imagined they could, even when the going was almost intolerable, can also potentially help you through challenging moments on your journey. Many of the stories told here are whole lives condensed down to just few lines. The outcomes are often incredible, but the reality of their daily strife can't be fully described in such a small space. In some cases it took individual women many years to see the fruits of their success.

Each individual journey has had its own timing and rhythm, and yours will be no different. Most of the stories recount situations other people have lived through after considerable mileage has already been covered in their lives, and they are so amazing that it would be easy to be overwhelmed by them. Don't be. They are just people who have been driven by powerful reasons. Each one was just an ordinary person who found reserves that no one expected; it wasn't always obvious what was under the surface until they started digging. It will be the same for you.

Use the stories to imagine where you might go yourself if every barrier was taken down. What could you achieve if you were told that anything was possible? What would you attempt then? Please don't use these amazing tales as a measure to judge your own past performance; instead, use them as a way for you to see what might be possible in your future. Start to write your own story. You can't change the past, so start from where you are now.

More than fifteen years have passed since my own "pack of bacon day", and life is thankfully, very different. To move from where I was then to where I am now, I have had to make many changes. Changes to how I work, what I do, but more than anything I have had to change how I think. I hope that I can play a tiny part in helping you to do the same.

We are naturally creatures of conflict. For women, a good deal of our conflict is internal. It is emotional. We are often torn between opposing needs. The needs of others and our own personal needs. We often have conflicting responsibilities too. Caring for children, keeping family together, being in a relationship, earning a living. These responsibilities often conflict with our own financial and emotional needs and hamper our ability to create financial self-reliance. We will cover how to overcome these conflicts later in the book.

There are lots of women who do find a happy balance. It is possible. But to 'have it all' is about finding alignment, balance and a level of freedom. All of that doesn't happen by accident. It takes work. You will need to do some careful design work to get the balance right. It IS worth the effort, and you can have fun and enjoy a real sense of achievement by finding that balance and doing the work.

I wrote this book to give you a guide that could help you to work your way through the complexities of modern life better equipped than ever before. To help you to find the answers to some of the questions that make navigating the route such a challenge at times. It is not always just about finding answers. Sometimes it is about learning to ask the right questions of yourself and of others. To do both of these things you need to know where to look, and knowing where to look is a skill in itself.

Getting good at knowing where to look is one of the skills that successful woman all master to some degree. We do it at home all the time; we always know where to look. That comes naturally to us. It's just a question of transferring that skill into some other areas of your life, and using it to find answers and not just socks! Here is one dictionary definition of the word 'skill':

An ability and capacity acquired through deliberate, systematic, and sustained effort to smoothly and adaptively carryout complex activities or job functions involving ideas (cognitive skills), things (technical skills), and/or people (interpersonal skills). See also competence.

Skills are where it's at. The skills to align your life, the skills to create a balance between others and yourself, the skills to manage your time, the skills to earn more money, the skills to keep more of your money, the skills to save money effectively, the skills to invest well and, last but NOT LEAST, the skills to channel your emotions and create your own unique brand of happiness.

Wealth is a skill. Happiness is a skill, and the great news is that anyone can learn a skill. You need the skills to manage your motivation, your emotions and your reactions to the inevitable setbacks. You even need skills to manage the success and money when it comes.

You can rest assured that all this is possible for you—wherever you are starting from.

Nine Things You Don't Need to Become Wealthy

"I think that the most important thing a woman can have
– next to talent, of course – is her hairdresser."
—Joan Crawford

I f you have any worries about your education, skills, background or abilities, it might comfort you to know a few things that were missing from my toolkit when I started.

I didn't start out in life with any particularly special skills. I admit that I have always had a degree of physical coordination, but not enough to take me to the top level of any sport (and I have tried!). I haven't always worked hard, or studied hard; however, I have increased my ability to do both as the years have rolled on. Do I have skills that you can learn too? Absolutely. In part because I copied a lot of the skills that have been useful to me from other people. Anyone can copy a system if they know how.

If you have a belief that you *still* haven't shaken off, that wealth is for a talented few, here are some facts about me that might provide you with some encouragement:

1. I have never been good with numbers. I failed Maths GCE. Badly.
2. I don't have any 'A' levels.
3. I don't have a degree.
4. I haven't built a massive business employing lots of people.
5. I never did climb to the top of a corporate greasy pole.
6. I don't come from a wealthy family.
7. I didn't marry a rich husband.
8. I flit, have a short attention span and have had more job changes than is considered normal by most people.
9. My CV reads like a horror story of inconsistency and is full of voids, strange jobs and weird business ventures.

There is a whole bunch of other things that I am rubbish at too. In short, I'm a fairly normal person. A run of the mill, ordinary woman.

And just so you know, I didn't make my money by just having one good idea, or doing one thing at a time, or even by doing any one thing for very long. I don't do *anything* for very long. I turned my tendency to flit into a constant stream of different money making activities. I turned that tendency on its head and made it work for me. I have created a series of little money making machines, and I have a lot of fun doing it.

I never get bored with my job. I never have one for long enough to get bored. Lady Gaga dropped out of college too (that made me feel better about only doing six weeks of college and moving on). She was worth over $50 million dollars the last time I looked. She didn't get a degree, but it obviously didn't hold her back, did it? She may have a talent, but there are lots of singers with talent, and that's my point. She had other skills too.

So if I can do it, if Lady Gaga can do it, **anyone** can. You need some skills, you need a clear purpose and you need belief. These are all available when you know where to look.

The Three Keys to Wealth

"All I ask is the chance to prove that money can't make me happy."
—Spike Milligan

How do you get out of debt and become wealthy?
There are three basic steps, and they sound simple if you say them quickly enough! First, you have to consciously develop a way of thinking, a wealth mindset if you like. Second, you have to manage your money well, starting with managing small amounts effectively while you learn your wealth-craft. Finally, you have to find out how to maximise your income until eventually your money takes over and starts doing more work than you do. So let's take an overview of what's covered in this book so you know what to expect from it.

First of all—Mindset. This is the focus of Section 1.

This part of the book is all about how to regain control over what goes on inside your own mind. Here you will uncover how to find your ideal life alignment, a sense of balance and your true purpose. Without those things, it's almost impossible for you to be effective or consistent. You need to have control over your thoughts and your behaviours around money. Here you will look head-on at your own values, beliefs and attitudes.

You need to realise up front that you can't *just* think your way to wealth. You will need to do some work, probably a lot of work! But you can work hard and end up not keeping any of your hard earned money if you don't have the right mindset. You have the capacity to have total and utter control over your own mind, and here you will learn some great ways to do it.

But here's the thing, if you are not in *conscious* control of what your own mind is doing, others have a level of control over you. You can either make up your own mind, what you think and choose your own destiny, or someone else will probably do it for you.

Once you start to develop the right mindset, you need to take full control over your outgoings. This is the focus of Section 2.

Although that sounds simple, there are forces that are fighting for your heart, mind and money every moment of every day. You will find out how wealthy women become masters over these forces. You will discover the practical tools to take control over your money. You will find out how to get out of debt, how to manage your money, and how to control any unwanted spending cravings as well.

Thirdly, you need to maximise your earning power. Making vast amounts of money and living an extravagant, millionaire lifestyle is beyond the scope of this book, apart from to say that to accumulate any level of wealth you will need to work hard at some point, and then invest the rewards wisely.

Inevitably, there is a cross over between all three because what goes on inside your head affects both how you manage your money and what you earn. Your thoughts though, stay at the centre of everything you do; that's why I have shared the value of your mindset with you first. You managed your pocket money when you were a kid, didn't you? When you ran out, there wasn't an infinite supply from your parents. You weren't given a credit card when you were eight! Life was simple. By the end of this book, you will have the tools to make things that simple all over again.

Thinking Your Way To Wealth

Stuck at a Crossroads?

"...I see myself at a crossroads in my life, mapless, lacking bits of knowledge – then, the Moon breaks through, lights up the path before me..."
—John Geddes, *A Familiar Rain*

How do some people manage to extricate themselves from difficult situations while others swirl around getting sucked deeper and deeper into life's problems?

We all have times when we get stuck at a crossroads in our lives. Times when the lights seem like they are stuck on red, but when standing still is not an option. When you can't just sit on the junction because there's a big truck coming right at you—and it's got no brakes. The truck might be the electricity bill, an overdraft, an illness or a relationship that sucks. Whatever the nature of the truck, it's thundering at you—and it's not slowing down. Does life ever feel like that for you?

When I was researching this book I listened to the experiences of many other women, and the word 'crossroads' came up more than any other. Considering this was a book about finance, that surprised me a little. It was obvious that it was a lack of clear direction that was a problem for so many people and a shortage of money was merely a symptom of that.

Women told me about their situations. Christie said, "I know I can't keep going like this, but I don't know which direction to take. If your book will help me make some decisions I want to read it!"

Janine said, "I'm at a crossroads, I don't know whether to go back to University and get the job I really wanted when I was younger, or to just keep my job I have working at the bank. I do OK, but I don't enjoy it. I feel like I can't afford to escape."

Paula told me, "I feel like I have drifted from job to job. I still haven't found what I want to do. I do know what I **don't** want to do though! The things I enjoy the most don't seem to make money. I love working with animals, but jobs with animals barely pay a living wage."

Nicky said, "I'm a lawyer, my parents were lawyers, it was always what I was going to do. No one ever asked me if it was what I wanted. I don't think I even asked *myself* if it was what I wanted. The job pays well but I'm not happy and nothing else I can think of will pay me the amount money I need. I hate the conflict of the law. It's all about fighting cases and it gets me down. I don't know what to do; I feel stuck."

Many of these women will drift along until something goes wrong. Until a job is lost and they run out of savings, or until they get pregnant and have to decide how much financial responsibility they can hand over to their partner; if there is a partner. Or until they make themselves ill with the stress. Or until they lose someone dear to them and realise that they wasted time doing things they didn't enjoy.

Opportunities have a habit of appearing at our biggest moments of crisis. There is a good reason why the most beneficial changes open up to you during the most difficult periods of your life. At times of crisis we are so often forced to act because of circumstances seemingly outside of our direct control. Personal difficulties, relationship breakdowns, financial disasters—all of these situations force change upon us. All the balls get thrown into the air. It is this state of disruption and flux that can change your perception for just long enough to allow you to view the situation from a different angle. Cosy familiarity is not an option at times like that. Difficult times disturb our world. They cause us to question our beliefs and assumptions. Difficult times give you the chance to make radical shifts to your thinking. They often provide new and powerful reasons for change. Difficult times give you a real reason to get off the fence.

At some point, everyone has to get off the crossroads. Not making a decision does have its own consequences. When you let go of blame (that includes blaming yourself), you can get out of the path of the speeding truck. That in turn can allow you to stop clinging to the comfort zone of what is familiar to you. The acceptance that what's familiar isn't always right, even if it is comfortable, is an essential part of change. It is often the case that trying to retain a status quo is what puts people onto the crossroads in the first place and standing in the path of that speeding truck.

If you don't have a current disaster, you can learn to use other tools to create the shifts you need to make artificially. That is one way for you to get yourself moving again so you don't get run over by the next truck.

Although I can't give you every answer, I can give you a process that you can apply to many of the life's financial challenges. However, I do know this: being paralysed by worry won't give you the impetus you need. Stress alone will not help you, it might be a catalyst (depending on your reaction to it), but you need more than that. You need new ways of doing things.

So how do you know if the direction you are taking now is the right one? The simple answer is that very often you don't! That very uncertainty is a reason why so many people stall before they even get going. They wait for the whole story, the whole journey to be mapped out before they start and that just isn't going to happen. There will be roadblocks, diversions, and things that slow you down. An important part of the process is to gain the courage to get moving *roughly in the right direction*, even before you know the final destination. You can worry about which way to turn at the next set of lights when you get there. Just move along the road one junction, and one set of traffic lights, at a time. If you pay attention you will see signs along the road.

You will get much further, much faster if you don't try to solve all your problems at once. Wealth doesn't work like that, and nor does life. It's all a process—not an event. If you are at a crossroads in your life right now, the answer will come to you when the time is right. In the meantime, look after your money as best you can so you can keep your head above water. We will get to the practicalities of that in Section 2. For now, let's keep focussed on all the good things you have going for you as a woman.

The Women's Century – It's Our Time

"A woman is like a tea bag – you never know how strong she is until she gets in hot water."
—Eleanor Roosevelt

Is it getting easier for women, or harder? Is juggling multiple responsibilities making it more complicated for women to be successful? I don't believe so. In fact, I think it is easier now than ever. I want you to take a moment to appreciate how much easier it is for you, because of the times you live in, than it has been up until now. However difficult things are for you at the moment, at least you don't have the law working against you. It hasn't always been like that. Consider the challenges that your grandmother and your great-grandmother faced.

I look back through my own family and see that my own grandmother worked, she had a job that she was passionate about, and she even kept her own money. That was a big deal back then. She did consider herself to be a bit of a revolutionary, and she drew a few raised eyebrows from the neighbours. Most the women who lived in her road were traditional stay-at-home wives. My other grandmother worked all of her life in a match factory. She lost her husband in the Second World War and had a family to support. She did what she needed to do, and her work gave her a strong identity and many loyal friends. But for that generation, there weren't many options open to women.

Women professionals in high paying jobs or running businesses were incredibly rare, and not very socially acceptable. Before the Second World War, most women were financially dependent on their husbands or families.

In your great-grandmothers' day, most women didn't even have the *option* of looking after their own financial security. That wasn't a choice they could make, even if they wanted to. Money in the family was under the control of someone else. That was not that long ago. Add that to the fact that the class system almost totally defined your great-grandmother's fate from the moment she was born.

Your great-granny had few choices about anything much at all. It is likely that the financial responsibility for her well-being came from within a family with a man at the helm. Either her husband if she was married or she may have been in service and paid a wage to look after someone else's family. Either way, the man at the helm of one family or another would have had control over almost every aspect of her life. If she was part of the true working class, she was likely to have worked in an industrial factory in harsh conditions, or maybe doing back-breaking work on a farm.

In almost every scenario women didn't generally have much power over their own lives. Freedom and choice wasn't on the menu. Even the upper classes with trust funds and estates were often married as part of an arrangement that preserved (or enhanced) the estate, the wealth or status of the two families involved. It was just the way that it was.

So how lucky are you?

It is amazing to realise just what is open to your generation. However difficult life may be for you now, you have opportunities that your grandmother couldn't have imagined.

You can educate yourself without fear. You can go to university. There are thousands of female doctors, lawyers, teachers and businesswomen. There are women lorry drivers, vets, social workers and journalists. The list of options that you have to engage in something useful and earn a living goes on and on. You can work from home. Some are making millions from home-based internet businesses. Why not you?

Women in previous generations died just to get the freedom to vote. Even in the UK it was impossible for women to get a degree until the middle of the 20th century in many universities. Well done to University College London who placed women on an equal footing from 1878. Without a degree, it was difficult to enter into a professional career. Have you heard the fascinating story of Dr Barry?

Doctor James Barry was born around 1789. Barry graduated from medical school in Edinburgh, and then worked at St Thomas' Hospital in London, before he joined the Army. A successful career as a surgeon followed, in both India and South Africa, and he eventually rose to the rank of Inspector General in charge of military hospitals. Impressive stuff. Barry's methods of nursing the sick and wounded soldiers in the Crimea gave his patients the highest recovery rate of the whole war.

He performed one of the first successful Caesarean sections in 1826. He went on to serve in Mauritius, Trinidad and Tobago, and on the island of Saint Helena. A very well-travelled officer, long before the days of planes and airports. Barry was opinionated, renowned for not being easy to get on with. He even got into an argument with Florence Nightingale! Despite all that, his continuing career saw him reach dizzy heights.

It was only when the distinguished doctor died of dysentery in 1865 that it was discovered "he" was in fact a she.

"He" was a woman called Margaret Ann Bulkley. Multiple towels wrapped under her clothes had hidden her curves for her entire 46-year career with the Army. Her faithful servant had kept her secret. He/she had been known for having an effeminate manner; it was hardly surprising. The British Army's response? They kept the records secret for 100 years.

In countries around the world, women are still dying for the freedoms we enjoy in the West. Take the case of Malala Yousafzai, the young girl from Pakistan who was shot in the head by the Taliban in October 2012. Her crime was blogging about the banning of education for girls. She just wanted to keep going to school.

Spare a thought for the thousands of women who die as a result of childbirth every year because they have no medical facilities. In the western world we have more opportunity and better health than women have had in any other time in history.

How lucky are we to be able to follow a passion and earn a living at the same time? We can marry for love. It may not make everything easy all of the time, but if you are educated well enough to be able read this, and have the time and inclination to do so, you are luckier than most women in the world.

It isn't that easy in India. Patricia Narayan married for love, but it was to someone branded as being from the "wrong" community. She was rejected by her family, and later her marriage went badly wrong. Her husband became a drug addict and an alcoholic. She was physically abused daily, and she was left alone with two young children.

She eventually found the courage to leave, and in desperation was sheltered by her disapproving parents. However, despite the fact they took her in, her father didn't forgive her. She was determined to be independent. She knew she couldn't live like that.

Patricia started selling coffee from a cart. She had always had a passion for cooking, so she prepared pickles, squashes and jams to sell from the cart too. It wasn't because she had ambition; she simply needed to make enough money to eat. Some days she came home crying, having sold hardly anything, but she kept going. Over time, she expanded the range she sold from the cart and her tiny little business started to do well. Patricia said in a recent interview, *"There was a fire in me that made me believe that I could be successful without anyone's help. I did not want to be a failure. If you have that fire, nothing in the world can stop you from succeeding."*

Years later, when her children had grown up, she tragically lost her beloved daughter in a car crash. Patricia was shattered by the accident. She handed the business to her, by now, adult son.

After a two-year break, he encouraged her back, and she returned to her business. As a tribute to her daughter, she provided an ambulance for future crash victims at the accident blackspot of her daughter's death. She wanted to help others, dead or alive, at the scene of road accidents. She didn't want any other mothers to watch ambulance staff refusing to take away a dead body from the scene of an accident like she had done. Her own daughter was removed in the boot of someone's car.

Patricia now employs 200 people and runs a chain of restaurants. What an inspiring woman. Take a mental note of the fact that Patricia's success came not from ambition, but from desperation. Motivation comes from the strangest of places. The fuel is different for each of us. We will come back to that.

Many future fortunes will be made not just by producing tangible "things", but from feeding minds and souls. In the western world, most of us have enough to eat. Materialism can only go so far. There are only so many TVs, cars and washing machines that we need. We are already almost at saturation point with mobile phones. I believe that women, with our natural tendency towards pursuing emotional fulfilment and caring for others, are perfectly positioned to lead this new style of wealth creation with a sense of contribution built in.

Until recently, information technology had the emphasis on the *technology*. It is at last moving towards the information itself being of the greatest importance. Because the technology side has an engineering and mathematical bias, it was dominated by men. Males do have a natural attraction to technology—to gadgets and computers. There aren't too many women nerds out there.

For a time I worked in IT, and it was certainly true that the technical side of the business attracted mostly men. They had a natural aptitude towards programming and logical thinking. Now I think that there has been a distinct shift towards the *information* itself. Content is king. And more and more content is being created to fulfil our emotional needs. Women are in a perfect position to take the lead here. Our opportunities have never been more exciting.

The modern world is becoming more about emotional strength, rather than pure physical strength. The tenacity, dedication and empathy that women have naturally are going to explode into the world like never before.

It is our time now.

Respect Your Money

"Money is always on its way somewhere. What you do with it while it is in your keeping and the direction you send it in say much about you. Your treatment of and respect for money, how you make it, and how you spend it, reflect your character."
—Gary Ryan Blair

Is your relationship with money a healthy one? Do you respect money or do you secretly fear it, or even hate it?

However useful it is to have a good budget, to pay your debts, to be motivated, or even to pitch a world-changing business idea, none of it will be much use to you if your thoughts about money are off kilter. You will only keep your money so that you can get it working for you if your attitude toward it is in good shape.

Your relationship with money has to be comfortable. Do you and money get on, or do you have a bit of a stormy relationship?

Do you attract money, or do you just grab at it when you get the chance? When I was really strapped for cash it used to feel like the more I needed it, the further away it got. Does that sound familiar? Over the years I have come to the conclusion that it is more like a human relationship than I ever imagined.

Here is one simple example. If you want to have enough money to own a house outright, but at the back of your mind you can't imagine having say £250,000 in cash (depending on where you live of course), you won't get it. Simple. That's what it takes to buy a nice house in a good area almost anywhere in the UK today. In some parts of the country it can be even more than that. Wherever you live, in whatever country you live, you will know what the number is, how much you would need. If you don't think that you will ever have that much in the bank, you are right! Your brain won't let you have it. You will drive it away. You need to get your relationship with money on the right track. You need to get your beliefs in line with your desires. That's because your beliefs are the essence of who you are. You need your outward reality to stay consistent with the *real you*. The you inside.

If you have niggling thoughts that millionaires are greedy people, and you don't consider yourself a greedy person, you will limit how much money you will let yourself have. You have to. You can't allow yourself to become a millionaire if that's what you think. You can't be greedy and not greedy at the same time. Your beliefs won't let you; it would cause to much internal conflict. You need to stay true to your beliefs.

That is why, before we got to this point, you have already read some inspirational tales of women who have already got what they want. That was deliberate. I wanted you to start to question some of your beliefs about possibilities right from the start.

These inspirational stories only really tell you about the *behaviours* of the women concerned. They only skim the surface. Behaviours will only show you so much, because they are external manifestations. Behaviours only let you see what people want you to see. Unless you know how to read them...

Addressing your own belief system is where the real gold is buried. Understanding how you think, then learning how to *choose* how you think is the **alchemy** for life. Because how you *think* is what drives how you *function*.

How you think, and what you think **about**, drives how you talk to yourself, and we ALL talk to ourselves. How you talk to yourself is also a pattern for how you talk to others. What you believe about yourself—and what you project outwards—because all of those beliefs will be consistent with all of your internal thoughts. And other people have a remarkable, natural skill for picking up on your beliefs and values. You broadcast it all, through your attitude.

What you believe constitutes who you are, and everything that you do will be consistent with that. If your beliefs are confused or conflicted, then there is a good chance that you will come across as appearing confused and conflicted to others. Or even worse, you may appear to have double standards. People have a talent for making wrong assumptions.

Other people will want to be with you—or not—because of what you think. They can't hear your thoughts, but because you always behave in a way that is consistent with those thoughts, you **do** project them outwards, even if you don't mean to.

To illustrate the point, can you think of anyone who comes across as insecure and needy but at the same time is a magnet who attracts other people? Money is the same. It gravitates towards people who already appear to have enough of it, or people that seem not to care about it. In the same way that popular people seem to attract friends when they have plenty already. I've seen it over and over again. The more I seemed to need money when I was broke, the faster it legged it in the other direction. Sound familiar?

Any healthy relationship only functions when both parties work together. Both players have a responsibility, not just to each other but to the relationship itself. The difference with your relationship with money is that you can't wait for money to change. Or force it to change. It won't. If you are struggling financially at the moment, you can't stay the same. If you do, your relationship with money is stuck in a rut. Something has to give.

You need to know how to make yourself attractive to money. You need to treat it with a new level of respect. For you to get on well with it, you have to like it enough to tolerate having it around! Cash needs to feel welcome, cared about, respected and treated well. If not, it will go somewhere else. To someone else who is prepared to put more effort into the relationship.

So take responsibility for your part in your relationship with money. Be respectful, and don't give off the desperate vibe. It's unattractive to men, women and money.

What Did You Inherit from Your Family?

"To enjoy good health, to bring true happiness to one's family, to bring peace to all, one must first discipline and control one's own mind."
—Buddha

So how does your background and family influence your financial outcomes? And how easy is it to move between economic tiers? Should we believe the politicians dire warnings about the difficulties of 'social mobility', or is it all tosh?

We are all influenced by the money attitudes of our parents. Some finance experts call this your "money script". We witnessed how money was used at home when we were kids. You will have seen your parents' attitudes to money and you will have been affected by it. That doesn't mean that you always do the same things as they did. Sometimes you may do the polar opposite just for the hell of it. Whichever way, the money script of your parents will have rubbed off on you.

Maybe your parents got by on as little as possible. Maybe they tried to get as much as possible. Maybe they didn't care too much as long as the bills were paid. Maybe they were generous, maybe they were stingy. Maybe they worried about money, maybe they were care free. Whatever their attitudes, they are always there, hovering like ghosts in the background. You were trained to think about money in certain ways when you were a child. You didn't think about it, your parents didn't think about it. It just happened; the same way as learning to walk just happened. So what did constitute your accidental "training"? Every family has "ways of doing things". Items that other kids had may have been nominated as being trivial or a "waste of money" by your parents. Especially when you were a teenager! You were almost certainly denied something that you wanted, something that your parents didn't agree with. You were probably desperate to have a toy, an item of clothing or an album that you couldn't get your hands on because they controlled the money. Their choices ruled. Their attitudes to money, and what it was spent on, were the law of the house. He who has the gold makes the rules. Your image of the road ahead was being defined for you at every turn. When you were a child, the value placed on items, the value placed on learning, on relationships and how you spent your time were setting the patterns of your own values for your adult future.

If you have kids of your own, you have the same power over them.

As we start to grow up and take over control of our choices from our parents, we start to claim the road ahead for ourselves.

"We are taught you must blame your father, your sisters, your brothers, the school, the teachers—but never blame yourself. It's never your fault. But it's always your fault, because if you wanted to change you're the one who has got to change."

—Katharine Hepburn

I remember listening to a friend complaining about his younger sister. William lived in a castle. Not a little castle, not a fake castle, not a house with little turrets on it, but a proper castle. A big one. With lakes, a moat, big studded oak doors, parklands, the works. There was even a few thousand acres around it to round things off nicely. The castle was full of furniture that had been passed down through generations. A host of treasured heirlooms that told the story of the family through the generations. William told me how his sister, Lucy, who was about twelve at the time, despised the furniture in her bedroom and was making a daily fuss about it. She was obsessed; she nagged morning, noon and night. She drove them all nuts, because Lucy wanted shiny new Ikea furniture. Just like her friends had.

She may well laugh about it now, 20 years later, but at the time she was deadly serious. There is nothing wrong with Ikea furniture, I might add. It just isn't built with furnishing a castle in mind. She was trying to make a statement that made her more like her friends. Ordinary friends that didn't live in castles. She was trying, in her own small way, to break away from the road map set out for her by her parents. She wanted to create her own set of values, and her bedroom was a good place to start.

Lucy thought that Ikea furniture in her bedroom would make her more popular with her friends. That's certainly one of the arguments she used to make her case. To her, at that time, it was an absolute reality. She created hell over it. She wanted to fit in. It was more likely that the castle was the problem, not her bedroom furniture. We will come back to peer pressure and pester power later. But the moral of that story is that Lucy's parents didn't buy cheap furniture. They valued quality and longevity. They didn't buy Ikea for her in the end either. It probably gave her a good incentive to earn her own money later in life. The desire for that furniture probably stayed with her for a long time.

We don't all inherit money or castles. But we do inherit many of our attitudes to our money and about our family home.

When I was a little girl, I remember my Grandmother buying a new car. Now that may not sound like a big deal to you, but in 1970 it was an event to be celebrated. Especially for a woman. Granny paid for her precious car herself with money that she earned from her job. Most families still only had one car, and it was usually the man who paid for it, and was in charge of it. Her beloved car was a gleaming white Ford Cortina. When she wasn't driving it, she stared lovingly at it from the window of the front room. She cleaned it to within an inch of its life. I'm surprised it had any seats left after the amount of elbow grease that went into polishing those leather seats.

I have a clear memory of her proudly telling me that if I worked hard, I could have anything that I wanted. I also watched how carefully she looked after it; after all, she had saved up for years to buy it—and it wasn't going to rack and ruin on her watch! She came from a family that struggled to earn every penny when she was a girl herself. Her mother often struggled to buy food. So you can see where she learned the value of money. It came from her mum. The appreciation got passed down.

They were useful attitudes to absorb when I was small: work hard and get what you want, then look after what you have worked so hard to get. When I bought my first pair of jeans (with my own money from a paper round) a few years later, I wouldn't even let Mum wash them, they were so valuable to me! I have looked after my purchases that way ever since—the way Granny looked after that boxy, adored white Ford. I didn't choose to think like that; it was almost bred into me.

As well as a useful lesson learned, my beliefs were partly formed by that car. I developed a deep seated and unshakable belief that when you work hard, and save, you deserve your reward. And with money saved up, when no one is damaged in the acquisition of it, there is no guilt required and no apologies to be made for having it. Granny worked hard, she helped people, she saved up and she deserved that car. The car was a symbol of the amazing fact that a woman could create her own reality, even when society was still grappling with the idea of women going to work.

So what were your family's attitudes to money? What surrounded you every day when you were growing up?

What chances of success would you give a poor black American woman born in the backwoods of Mississippi to a single teenage mum? Someone who was raped at nine years of age, then, at the age of 14, gave birth to a son who died shortly after he was born? You might not think her start in life would make her a likely candidate for a billion dollar fortune. Yet that girl was Oprah Winfrey. Her start in life was almost one of unimaginable hardship, but it didn't stop her becoming one of America's most successful women.

It doesn't matter if you were good at school or not. It doesn't matter if you came from a difficult family situation or not.

Oprah didn't end up poor, despite her start in life. If academic achievement wasn't your strong suit, there are plenty of examples of people who left school without an exam to their name; some who could barely read or write have gone on to extraordinary levels of success. Richard Branson is dyslexic and struggled at school. He had a poor academic record, but it didn't stop him.

Mary Kay Ash didn't go to college, but she was one gutsy lady. And a self-made millionaire many times over. She has been named as the most successful businesswoman in American history. Mary wrote a marvellous book about her life and building her business. Although it looks old fashioned in our modern world (dresses at home—never trousers!), her attitudes to getting things done are timeless.

If you come from a wealthy family, you are more likely to have collected useful information about the process of making money, managing it and growing more of it. You are likely to have the belief that it is possible to make more. That's useful, but it is far from essential. If you were brought up with very large amounts of money, you will already be acutely aware that there can be problems in that scenario too.

People from rich families are still at risk of picking up unhelpful attitudes. Just think of the unhappy children of so many wealthy stars (Cher, the late Farah Fawcett, Judy Garland's daughter Liza Minnelli, etc.). For the kids of these women, money was no object; however, they have all struggled with addictions or personal problems that none of us would want.

If you have kids of your own, what money attitudes are you passing onto them? It's worth thinking about. You have a duty to educate them so they can look after themselves financially when they grow up. A basic financial education and healthy respect for money is far more important than going without so you can give them expensive presents.

I came from a family without much money. My mother went cleaning to make sure I could go on school trips and have shoes that fitted me as I was growing up. The most important thing she passed to me was ambition. If your parents didn't pass that onto you, it's not an excuse to not to start now!

The relevant question is this. If you have not inherited the belief that money is abundant from your family or your environment, what can you do about it now?

First of all, you need to re-think your beliefs and any negative emotional reactions that you have inherited about money. If you don't, your subconscious will drive you away from it. Some of the negative values and beliefs we have about money (and I believe that we all have some), will have come directly from our parents. If your parents argued about money within earshot, you will have picked up plenty of negative associations. It might be that money equals stress, or money equals conflict. If money came in easily but never stayed around, you might have grown up thinking that it was easy to get but not easy to keep. The combinations are endless, but each family has its own unique set of associations to money.

The book *Rich Dad, Poor Dad* is a very insightful book on this subject. If family attitudes to money is something that interests you, I recommend it.

Just remember that the attitudes to money you absorbed growing up, you picked up by accident. You didn't seek them out. Now that you are older, it is time to pick some up deliberately. Because if you are reading this, I can make an educated guess that all is not right in your bank account at the moment. If your attitudes *stay* accidental, there is a good chance that your finances are accidental too. They might even be an accident waiting to happen, or maybe the truck has already hit!

We are all influenced by our families and our early experiences of money. It is my firm belief that we can choose the future, wherever we came from. As adults, our greatest gift is that we get to choose what we believe and how we behave. That does extend to our finances. Get deliberate about your attitudes to money. Not everything you inherit is valuable to you. Recognising that is a good start.

Your Powerhouse — Your Values

"Here are the values that I stand for: honesty, equality, kindness, compassion, treating people the way you want to be treated and helping those in need. To me, those are traditional values."
—Ellen DeGeneres, comedienne

So what are your values? And why do they matter?

Values are the moral principles that guide your life. Your values are your accepted standards of behaviour, your ethics, and they guide almost every decision you ever make. Your values are your sense of right and wrong. Of what is fair and what is unfair. You won't always be aware of them, but they are there, lurking in the back of your mind ready for use whenever you have to make a *value judgement.*

They are the standards that you set for yourself, and any contradictions will result in a strong sense of discomfort, or emotional imbalance of some sort. Your values also provide boundaries for your beliefs and behaviours.

Imagine that just for one day, you are allowed to do whatever you want with no further consequences. You have full immunity, nothing will ever happen to you. You won't be put in prison, and no one will ever find out. The day goes like this. Read on, and see how comfortable you are.

You are short of money, so you go to a bank and rob it. Remember, you will never be caught and no one will ever know. The customers in the queue look terrified, a little old lady faints. You don't have time to be nice so you scream at the lady behind the counter to hand over the money. You take a wad of cash, and sashay back into the sunshine leaving a room full of scared and angry people behind you.

Did that sit comfortably with you? Could you have actually done it, knowing that there would be no negative consequences? Or did you squirm just imagining it?

Did you feel uncomfortable about causing the old lady to faint? About stealing? Most people could never do it. It betrays too many of their own values. Reading that, your reaction is a clear demonstration of your values in action. Your inner principles will have made just visualising the scene uncomfortable for you.

Your values drive your decisions. That's why people (especially women) can't sell a product they don't believe in for very long, just to make a living. If you have no choice, your stress levels go through the roof and you may even get sick. Your values dictate what you can or can't do for a living, without being conflicted and guilty. Your values are what you measure things against. They dictate how important certain things are to you. "Strong family values", a term much used by politicians, is a nice woolly one. Every listener relates to the term "family values" in a different way. The defining value might be love, it might be loyalty, it might be security or nurturing. These are all specific values that drive your decisions. You have to understand your values to create true wealth. They drive your belief and behaviours towards charity, towards taxes. They sit there in the background, guiding most of the decisions you make, about almost everything you do.

It is critical to your success that you have control over your belief system. If violence goes against your values, you aren't going to be able to make your fortune by selling weapons. Your values just wouldn't let you do it. There is no way you could provide leadership in any situation where there is a fundamental contradiction between your values and your actions.

Many core values were collected along the way as you grew up. What, or who, shaped your values? Few of us overtly choose our values. Like our attitudes to money, we inherit many of them without even realising. Wherever they came from, your core values make up your inner principles and the standards by which you measure yourself, and by which you measure others.

Your values are the essence of your identity, and you need to be consistent with them. Your values dictate what you choose to believe.

Becoming wealthy is not about changing your values. That's selling out. Becoming wealthy is about making sure that your core values aren't compromised while you take the action required to get wealthy.

When you act in line with your values, you will have a sense of alignment, balance and purpose in your life.

The Beauty of Beliefs

"If you stumble about believability, what are you living for? Love is hard to believe, ask any lover. Life is hard to believe, ask any scientist. God is hard to believe, ask any believer. What is your problem with hard to believe?"
—Yann Martel, Life of Pi

Are you beliefs set in stone, or can they be developed to ease your journey?

Sitting quietly below your values, are your beliefs. Your beliefs flow out from your values. They are the emotions and the thoughts that reflect who you are. They reflect your deeper values and have the ultimate power to deliver your financial dreams. They can also stop them in their tracks. "You have to believe," you hear the gurus say; but believe what exactly? What if your dreams and your beliefs are poles apart?

Let me share some important things about beliefs with you. First of all, your beliefs tend to be evidence based. But here's the thing: they can be wrong! Most of us get a little indignant when we are told that our beliefs can be wrong, so let's dig a bit deeper. Suspend your beliefs for a moment.

Your core values, the principles that you live by, guide your personal beliefs about money, and about your relationship with it. There are so many beliefs about money to choose from; you will naturally gravitate towards ones that align with the standards that you set for yourself. Ones that appear to align with your core values.

When you aren't happy in a situation, especially when you aren't getting the results you want, or when you aren't enjoying the process of generating money, something is out of sync. The fact that your outcomes aren't what you want is the proof of the misalignment. So how do you know what is *out?* How do you get back into line?

We have all probably picked up beliefs along the way that don't serve us. If yours don't serve you, it's probably time to re-evaluate them. They may have even been passed through to you by someone else for their own gain. That's not as uncommon as you might think. It happens every day. Take one example, let's look at holidays.

I like to travel, but the idea that going on a sunshine holiday every year is somehow a basic necessity of life is a good example of a belief implanted by the tourist industry. It just doesn't follow that everyone needs that to go on holiday to be happy. Even the UK Office for National Statistics claims that almost 30% of people in Britain are unable to afford even a week's annual holiday. It uses a family's ability to afford a summer holiday as a measure for assessing poverty. Give me a break! This "shocking" holiday statistic was part of a wider report comparing levels of poverty and social exclusion. What a ridiculous measure. I know it's nice to go on holiday, but when I couldn't afford one for five years, I didn't starve or feel socially excluded. We are peddled this comparative rubbish day in and day out. Be careful what, and who, you believe. Take care what you absorb.

Choose your beliefs. Don't let some government agency, paid for with your tax bill, tell you what makes you poor or socially excluded. You really don't need a group of policy wonks to tell you what you should do with your hard-earned time off, so they can compare you to the Joneses. Don't believe the advertising agency folks either!

What if you believe that hard work will always get you everything you want? I think that with that belief you are destined to be disappointed. Because hard work alone is not enough. Ask anyone who works a 60 or 80 hour week in a sweat shop.

If hard work alone was enough, nurses, factory workers and junior doctors would all be wealthy. How does that work if you are on the minimum wage? Something is wrong with that. It doesn't add up. You will never be a millionaire, no matter how hard you work. Your belief system would need to shift for your outcomes to add up. Of course you need to work hard, but the belief that hard work is all you need to do is faulty. It's not that you need to change your beliefs; it's more that you need to add a few to make the ones you already have effective for you.

These beliefs and attitudes can be like an invisible rope tying your hands behind your back. Some of them will have been in your family, some of them come from your culture, and some of them come from the media. How many resonate with you?

Here are a just a few of the common beliefs that hold people back:

- Rich people aren't very nice
- Rich people are greedy
- Other people don't like the rich
- The more money people have, the more problems they have
- Rich people are dishonest
- Having too much money is sinful
- Having a lot of money is unfair
- Rich people lay themselves open to more criticism than ordinary people get
- Money is the root of all evil
- You can't have everything
- Being rich won't make you happy
- There is more to life than money
- More money brings more stress
- Money causes more problems than it solves

Some of these statements are as old as the hills. And they are ALL generalisations.

Before we look at any specific ones, it is worth understanding a bit more about language and how the words that we use shape our behaviour more than most people are aware of. Not grand language, not the weasel words of politicians, but the daily language that we use for normal communication.

If you look at the list again, you will see that some of those statements are so broad that they almost sound plausible. That's why they stick. That is why politicians talk about aspiration rather than about wealth. It is culturally acceptable to agree that aspiration is good, but that wealth is more questionable. That is total rubbish of course. Generalisations that loose are lazy. They are a handy shortcut for people with an agenda. There is a huge gap between the plausibility of a statement, between common "truths" and fact.

Here is one political classic, the sort of statement that can distort the money associations that you have: *"We need an economy that builds long term wealth creation, fairly shared."*

That doesn't make much sense, even though the sentiment sounds plausible. Think about it: how can anyone be incentivised to create wealth and at the same time, share it with the nation? What's fair about that? Such ridiculous statements affect us all. That guy got a standing ovation for that speech! It is just one example of how a pairing of statements can make an overall message seem reasonable, to the point that we don't question the truth of it. We are constantly bombarded by such weasel words, and they have a powerful effect on our associations and resulting beliefs about money.

Effective beliefs, ones that will serve you are carefully chosen, not just absorbed from jerks like the politician who wants something from you. The politicians just want your vote, so they can take your money away later. Choose beliefs that will produce the results that you **want.** Ones that won't compromise your values.

The press is another faction who wants to gain your agreement, loyalty and your money; they love to attack the rich when they have their own agenda (an agenda that will probably be kept secret from you). It happens all the time. A couple of favourites in the press about the rich are stories of greed and laziness. Saying that being rich is associated to laziness or greed is no more accurate than saying that all women are weak, and just as insulting. Saying that all rich people are greedy is no better than saying that all people on benefits are lazy. And yet, it is much more socially acceptable to brand the rich with a negative stereotype than it is to brand the poor as being lazy. The rich are an easy target. If you are going to be rich, you might as well know that in advance.

Most of these generalisations are utterly ridiculous when you examine them fully. And yet, some of them are so engrained in our culture, families and politics that we treat them as if they were real. To escape from the traps that are set for your thinking, and your resulting outcomes, you need to start to think for yourself. Stop having the associations that other people—people who want power over you—want you to have for **their own** benefit. You need to start thinking for your own benefit. Then you can do some good with your money.

You may have known somebody when you were young that came from a family with money who wasn't a very nice person, or behaved in ways that didn't make you feel comfortable. That would back up a generalisation about rich people that you have been exposed to elsewhere. When you are a kid, you generalise. That is one of the ways that children learn to make sense of the world. It would be too complicated a place to comprehend otherwise. The trouble begins when these oversimplified ideas get stuck in your mind. These generalisations can gradually solidify and become beliefs. Instead of questioning the idea, you start to believe it—to treat it as if it were real.

The older you get, the less you have time to challenge the little ideas that make up who you are. Even the smallest idea can end up as a solid belief that your brain notices every little reinforcement for, every piece of evidence you notice tells you that you can carry on believing. The scientists call it "confirmation bias",[1] and it's powerful stuff. It's not deliberate. It is just how we get through life. We use generalisations to reduce complexity.

How would it affect your ability to generate wealth for yourself and your family if you had a deep-seated belief that all rich people were greedy? Be careful what you end up believing.

Have you ever noticed that when you, or someone close to you, buys a different car, how many cars of the same model and colour that you suddenly notice on the road? I bought a silver Freelander recently (dealer mileage, one year old, paid in cash—remember that, we get to why I buy cars that way later). Now I see them everywhere. There are hundreds of the things. I had never noticed them before. I see silver Freelanders are everywhere. It's the same with your attitudes to money as it is with the car. You take notice of things that reinforce your early thoughts. That's confirmation bias in action. If you think rich people are greedy people, every time you see someone in the press who has ripped others off to get their riches, it will reinforce your belief that rich people are greedy. That's confirmation bias too. It will easily slip into your mind and become a generalisation. It's not a great leap to start thinking that ALL rich people are greedy. You would hardly notice a rich person who wasn't greedy. It wouldn't be on your radar to look out for one. You probably wouldn't know what to look for. Even if you did recognise one, your rule of rich-equals-greedy could be validated by that person being "the exception that proves the rule".

These are how our beliefs turn into convictions. And you need to start addressing the habit (a human habit) of fixing your beliefs, if you want more money. You can collect the beliefs you need to be a success along the way. As human beings, we do that all the time. It's time to start choosing your beliefs, rather than letting your beliefs be like a parasite, sucking away at your earning power.

Here's the stark fact about beliefs: a belief is simply a confidence in a "truth".

A belief is NOT a truth in itself. Your beliefs aren't truths. They are just a confidence that something is right. No one believed you could put a man on the moon, until someone did. The belief and the truth were not the same thing. At one point in our history, people believed the world was flat. It took evidence before people changed their beliefs. These days, with over-whelming evidence that the earth is round, people universally accept it.

So why is all this talk of the differences between beliefs and truths important to you?

Even if your core values are solid, but you are struggling with money issues, there is a chance that your current beliefs don't serve you very well.

We all have a tendency to look for evidence to support the beliefs we already have. We all have strong filters in our attention to make sure that we pick up signals that confirm we are right in our thinking. You will do it too. We all do it. It's what comes naturally. We gravitate towards people with similar interests because they support our beliefs in a certain area of our lives. We don't just want to talk about our interest with them; we want to validate our beliefs. We want to prove our area of interest is worthy of our attention. We want to reinforce our beliefs at every turn.

Your beliefs, the supposed truths about the world and yourself that you hold so dear, could just be plain wrong in some areas. Just realising that opens up new possibilities for you. Although you are entitled to believe anything you want, the important question is this: do your current beliefs about money or yourself help you or hinder you?

You may have a whole bunch of beliefs about money that severely hinder you. You may have beliefs about yourself that are even worse. If you want to be a success then you need to work out which ones help you and which ones block you. Be careful about your beliefs, and just remember you can choose them; don't let them choose you.

Get Free from Belief Bondage

"Whatever the mind can conceive and believe, it can achieve."
—Napoleon Hill, Think and Grow Rich

C an you change your beliefs? If you can, how does it help? Will changing your beliefs change your outcomes?

These questions are about you. Not your beliefs about the world around you, but about yourself. The beliefs that have the power to limit your abilities, or liberate them. The beliefs that are based on your experience, upbringing and self-generated evidence.

It might interest you to know that much of the evidence on which we base our beliefs about ourselves is contaminated. It's not just our beliefs about the outside world that can be wrong. The ones about ourselves can get badly distorted, too. A good deal of what we believe about ourselves can be based on what we imagine others think about us. That is a form of mind reading. And unless you are Derren Brown, you are probably very wrong about what other people think about you a good deal of the time.

Your beliefs should be things that you can depend on, that way they can serve you. Basing your opinions on what you guess that others think of you is a pretty sandy foundation on which to build your self-worth. Don't confuse what you imagine people think about you with the truth. It's a bad idea to base your beliefs about yourself on your perceptions of the imagined opinions of others. Most people are way too interested in themselves to have an opinion about you that matters very much anyway. That might be hard to accept sometimes, but it is true.

When you start to come to terms with the reality that people care about themselves a lot more than about what **you** wear or what **you** say, you unchain yourself. Instead of being shackled by such tosh, you can get started on becoming what you want to be instead.

In the UK there is a deadpan comedian called Jack Dee. In his autobiography he relates the story of the night that he finally gave up trying to be what he *imagined* other people would find funny but clearly didn't. He had been struggling away in the comedy clubs in London for quite a long time. He wasn't exactly top billing. He was waiting tables, and then at the end of his shift he did stand-up comedy and had food thrown at him. He was on the verge of giving up. In his case, he didn't just imagine what people thought about him; he knew. They shouted at the stage every night, or just got bored and talked through his act. He had evidence-based beliefs that stacked.

Jack Dee was right on the edge. One night he went on stage with the sole intention of telling the audience that this would be his last night of misery for everyone concerned. He went on stage ready to tell them what he thought about them, and the whole dreadful experience of trying to be a comedian. He was fully intending to tell them to get lost and that he wouldn't be back. Audiences had made his life hell, and he wasn't going to do it anymore. He went on stage and did exactly what he had promised himself he was going to do. With his (now famous) cynicism in full flow, his bitterness about the sheer awfulness of his experience of being a comedian just poured out.

He brought the house down. Instead of guessing what he thought people would find funny, for the first time, he played himself. The audience loved it, and Jack Dee found his unique "angle". The irony is that it had been there all along. When he stopped imagining what he *thought* people wanted, and played himself, his career took off. It wasn't his comedy that was off before that. He had been trying too hard (and failing) because of his false perception of what other people had wanted. He had been trying to second guess, when all along they just wanted the real person.

Such is the power of putting your mind-reading skills aside. It is a bit crazy to imagine that you can read the thoughts of others, and then behave as if they were real. And yet, most of us do exactly that most of the time. Do you? If you answered yes, now would be a good time for you to stop doing it! It is like hitting yourself in the face with a brick. You wouldn't hurt yourself like that, so stop doing it to your feelings too. It's madness.

Women are especially prone to this brand of mind reading. We are especially good at imagining what other people might be thinking and turning it into some sort of odd internal reality. I taught myself to laugh every time I catch myself doing it. As the years go by, I do it less and less and am a lot happier and more effective because of it.

So can you change your beliefs? Not quite as many people challenge their own beliefs as you might think. My view is that this is partly because it takes a concerted effort and, partly, because many people don't know they can. Changing your beliefs takes bravery, and it proves that you are flexible and creative. In fact, it actually makes you more flexible and creative, the more practice you get. If you want to be more successful than you are now, you have to have some behavioural flexibility. Flexibility is an important characteristic of the wealthy.

Really strong beliefs can become convictions.

I like the word convictions. Think of the phrase "the courage of your convictions" (that tells you how strong they can be). They can give you courage, but they can also imprison you. You wouldn't want to be *trapped* by your beliefs, would you?

What do you believe about yourself?

What beliefs you will come out of this process with will be totally unique to you. And so they should be. There is no point in trying to be someone else. It didn't do Jack Dee any good, did it? But there is a point in trying to be the person you want to be in the future. You do not have to stay who you are now forever. You don't have to put up with some of the things that you have to tolerate at the moment forever either. I heard someone say recently, "What you put up with is what you end up with." Think about that.

Getting the life you want will, in all probability, involve changing yourself in some way. It's not so scary though.

Are you the same person that you were last year, five years ago or ten years ago? I didn't think so. You can give yourself permission to keep developing. You can allow your beliefs to change at the same rate as you do, and be OK about it. It's not selling out; it's growing up. So the conclusion has to be this: of course you can change your beliefs!

So let's start looking more deeply into your beliefs and attitudes towards money.

Unleash a Great Attitude

"Your attitude, not your aptitude, will determine your altitude."
—Zig Ziglar

C an you touch an attitude? Can you buy one? Can anyone give you a new one for your birthday?

I guess you have answered those questions for yourself as you read each one, so you already know the answers. But what if there is more to it than a simple yes or a no?

Attitude is an easy word to say, but it's not so easy to put your finger on an attitude in real life. So what are they, where do they come from, can you choose them, and why does it matter anyway?

Your attitudes are a viewpoint. They are an orientation mechanism; they are the glasses through which you look at the world. They are also one of the mechanisms that we all use to compare ourselves to others in the world around us. They are one of the first things that people see about you. We can all see someone with a confident attitude from a fair distance away. We can all sniff arrogance and detect humility. All attitudes.

Your attitudes are not the same as your beliefs. Your attitude is how other people SEE your beliefs. It is through your attitude that you display your values and beliefs to those around you.

You can have a good or a bad attitude. You hear it all the time; a common one is listening to teachers talk about kids in their care. "He may not be the brightest, but he has a great attitude", or "she has a brain the size of a planet, but a bad attitude; what are we going to do about it?"

I bet I know which kid you would rather teach!

"Nothing can stop the man with the right mental attitude from achieving his goal; nothing on earth can help the man with the wrong mental attitude."

—Thomas Jefferson

On the days when you feel positive, you present a positive attitude to the world, and you can deal with anything that gets in your way. On the bad days, it's hard to keep an upbeat attitude. Your attitude is on display more than your skills. Every good leader knows that. Every leader pays as much attention to their attitude as they do to their knowledge. Every successful parent does the same.

Arrogance is an attitude; humility is an attitude.

To stay aligned with your core values and your beliefs, your attitude needs to display who you are and what you stand for. People who have developed that balance of views that have gone to the effort to develop the ability to show their beliefs through their attitude give out a good vibe. They show congruence. Other people trust people who are aligned well, people who are congruent. That's almost a definition of a good attitude. Congruence - truth - transparency. People like it when they know what they are dealing with.

Even if people don't like everyone with a good attitude, they do tend to respect it.

If your attitudes are built on the foundation of faulty (earth is flat) beliefs, then you aren't going to do yourself any favours.

You already know that your behaviours are driven by your values and that they are consistent with your beliefs; now you know that they are delivered with an attitude that reflects all of them. It's a fundamentally honest way to live. A good way to get wealthy. There is a clarity about people with a good attitude. If they are positive, and really mean it, there is an infectious quality about that. One that is universal. You can often see someone with a good attitude without even speaking or listening to them.

They are the ones who smile as you get on the tube. They are the ones serving you in a shop who look you in the eye and give an impression that they actually LIKE being with people. You don't need to be rich to have a good attitude. But if you do have one, you are much more likely to GET rich.

If you come from a background of financial hardship, or from a family that muddled along to get by (which would be most likely, as that is what most modern households do), you will have some inherited attitudes. And not all of them will serve you very well.

But let's be crystal clear about this. I have already demonstrated that you don't need to have come from a wealthy background to make money. And coming from a background with lots of it doesn't guarantee it either. Money won't make you happy on its own.

So why am I asking you to analyse your attitudes. Why bother?

Well, it is simple. You don't deserve a life of hardship. It is just so unnecessary. It **is** worth the trouble. Having values that are true to what you stand for, supported by beliefs that help you and don't damage others, plus a set of healthy attitudes to money, will allow you to have a healthy relationship with it. And healthy balanced relationships are happy relationships.

The aim of the game is to have your values, beliefs and attitudes aligned in a way that allows you to think and act in ways that help you. To allow you to be productive. And not to feel guilty when money lands in your bank account. It will also allow you to keep hold of enough of it. You have to be comfortable about having it—not just getting it. That is essential if you want the long term security of having *enough*.

You now know that in order to get the results you want, and those results are different from the ones you are getting at the moment, you will need to behave in different ways. You will need to take actions that are different from your usual pattern. You need to travel down a different road. You need to display to others that you want to do things differently now, and you do that by working on your attitude.

Attitudes Towards the Rich

"You can't have a good day with a bad attitude, and you can't have a bad day with a good attitude."
—Unknown

How do you perceive people who *already* have plenty of money? Do you have a strong reaction to the wealthy people you see on TV or read about in magazines? Are your emotions and attitudes about money, and people who already have it, in conflict with each other?

If you have a negative attitude about money, and people with money, do you that think you are likely to get more money—or less?

So I'll ask the question again, how do you react when you see people with lots of money? Many people have a subtle, yet strong, reaction. That is how media moguls make so much money! Ironic, isn't it? The very organisations that slate those with money are the same ones that get so much of yours...

People are fascinated by what other people have, how they make it, and what they do with it after they have got it. It is one of the ways we calibrate our own success, our own current place or standing in the world.

There is a massive industry built around successful people. And just as big an industry (if not even bigger) that is built around charting their downfalls. Maybe it is because so many people who don't take responsibility for their own outcomes feel a little better about themselves when someone who has done well comes unstuck. It is a sad fact that it is not enough for people to do well—they need someone else to do less well in order for their success to measure up. It's summed up well in the old saying "it's not enough for me to succeed, everyone else must fail."

The press thrives on such stories. Just look at Britney Spears. She was a press darling on the way up. Now she is hunted by them, they are enthralled by her difficulties, and the public buys this stuff!

When you read about a wealthy person (say Dame Mary Perkins who co-founded Specsavers, Jacqueline Gold, Victoria Beckham—a few names to get you started), how do the images of these people make you feel? Maybe you have never paid much attention to your own reactions before. Do you feel envious, excited, inspired? Or do you feel a sense of injustice? Do you feel distance or impossibility? Do you feel admiration or respect? Or a complex and confusing combination all of them with a few other emotions thrown into the mix? Start to pay attention from now on.

Maybe you feel very little. If you had a neutral reaction, you are a very rare person indeed.

If you currently have negative feelings, however subtle, about any aspect of wealth or the wealthy, you are going to struggle to get wealth of your own.

These are you attitudes, a two way mirror to your mind, at work. You need to start to expose your previously hidden (or not so hidden) beliefs about money and wealth. Begin to explore what these things currently represent to you. How they make you feel. That little exercise would be a good start.

If you are asking yourself why is it so important to know, let me give you some insight. The reason is this: whatever you do, you won't be able to act against your own internal value system. Remember that your attitudes reflect your beliefs, and your beliefs reflect your values. However hard you try. If you have mixed feelings about what money represents, your actions towards it will be mixed up too.

If you don't know what your deep-seated beliefs and values amount to, and your actions are being driven by them anyway, then you are being driven by an invisible hand that you can't control. The spooky thing is that invisible hand is your own! And you could be trying to work with it tied behind your back.

We all bring baggage about money into our adult lives from our upbringing, families, peer group and surroundings. If you are currently dealing with financial challenges that you want to break free from, there is a good chance you need to rebuild some of your thinking, some of your beliefs, and dump some excess baggage. Excess baggage costs a fortune, as anyone who has ever flown with a 'low cost' airline will tell you. Travel light. Only carry the good stuff around with you.

When you read a negative story about a rich person in the papers, remember to check your own reactions. Don't react how the jealous journalist who wrote the piece wants you to react. Don't get sucked into the negative attitudes of others.

That is one of the secrets of wealth.

The Great Female Balancing Act

"Happiness is not a matter of intensity but of balance, order, rhythm and harmony."
—Thomas Merton

S o what is real balance? How do you find it? How do you know when you have it, and how does it affect your wealth?

Life is a balancing act. Our modern lives seem to get increasingly complicated. It can be like living on a high wire. For women, I believe that it is more difficult to balance our lives than it is for men. We have so many things to balance: relationships, children, relatives, work, looking after our homes, taxes and more. I am sure your own list is huge.

At least money isn't complicated. Money is like calories. If you put more money into your purse than you take out, you purse gets fatter. If you take out more money than you put in, your purse gets thinner. Simple. Money does not judge. It doesn't care if we have done the housework or not. It just *is*. It doesn't have an opinion. It doesn't worry, and it certainly doesn't worry about you!

Just being rich is no more a guarantee of happiness than being married is a guarantee of being in love. To have lots of money without the values and appreciation that goes with it is like being married without being in love. To some people the daily reality of either one is just not what they had expected.

Do you believe that being married is a passport to happiness, or do you think that love is important too? A marriage certificate is just a bit of paper. It is not a happiness voucher. Money is just paper too. And piles of cash are not happiness vouchers either. In fact, if you don't have your emotional balance sheet balanced before you start building up your money, those bank notes can become misery vouchers too. That's the difference between being rich and being wealthy. Riches don't guarantee happiness. To me, wealth is a different thing altogether. There isn't just monetary wealth; you can have a wealth of friendships, a wealth of knowledge too. That's why I talk of wealthy women throughout, not "rich women".

There are plenty of sad characters on the "Sunday Times Rich List" who get divorced, overdose and have dysfunctional families. Does being simply rich help? Evidence suggests not. To be truly wealthy is to have wealth of emotion, experience and empathy that allows you to enjoy what you have become on the road to getting it.

There is a price to getting things and a just cost to NOT getting things. Like not getting your bills paid on time, or bouncing a payment at your bank. The price of these can often be disproportionate to the offence. It is best if you use your budgeting and planning skills to avoid those costs, because they aren't value for money. You are going to be working for yourself from now on, not for the banks.

To be happy with wealth, you need a balance sheet for your money and a balance sheet for your emotional and physical well-being too.

A "balance sheet" in financial terms is a simple snapshot of assets (things you own) presented on the left, minus liabilities (things you owe or have ongoing responsibility for, including your own drawings) on the right. A financial balance sheet needs to do just that: balance.

You may recall the day when I first did mine, it had 15p on the left and minus £60,000 on the right. My financial balance sheet represented the chaos in the rest of my life up until that point. There had been no balance in my life, and it showed.

You can quickly create an emotional balance sheet for yourself. If you are serious about getting wealthy, you can start right now. If you are in the mood and have the time, you can try this.

List all the good feelings you will have when you achieve what you want to achieve. You can include the impact of your success on others here too. Then list all the bad feelings you will have if you don't try. List the bad feelings that you want to get away from too. Anything which helps you to weigh up the emotional consequences and potential benefits.

What you are doing is starting to programme yourself that doing nothing is not an option. Because it really isn't. You have to do something, so you may as well get wealthy. The only other choice is to work hard to pay your bills, and make someone else wealthy at the same time.

We have all seen plenty of rags to riches stories; there are plenty in this book. But what about stories that go the other way? The reverse stories happen when people don't have their emotional balance sheet mapped out ahead of time. That's why wealth takes preparation.

Take the case of Alex Toth who won $13 million on the Florida lottery in 1990. Alex and his wife Rhoda could not even afford mains electricity before their windfall. But they had no money management skills before they won, and they demonstrated that they didn't have any afterwards either. After various spending sprees and other antics, they eventually split up, and at one point, Alex checked himself into a mental institution. By April 2008, Alex Toth was dead. He never made it to court to answer charges of not paying his taxes. Now, $13 million may be a lot of money (even if you opt to take it in instalments of $660,000 a year for 20 years like Alex did), but he isn't even still here to tell us if that lottery ticket was worth the price. *Everything* comes at a price. You need to prepare. Getting wealthy should take time. It's better that way.

Becoming wealthy isn't right for everyone. For some, the emotional cost and emotional energy required is just too draining. Focussing on things outside the family is just more than some women want to do.

There is no doubt that some of your energy will have to go outside the family if you want total financial independence. You need to decide if the balance is right for you. If you don't want to get truly wealthy, if you decide that the price is too high, you can get very comfortable and remain in balance personally. If you simply manage your finances well, spend less than you earn and save diligently, you can be financially secure, and for many people, that is enough. So what is enough for you?

What is Enough?

"Be thankful for what you have; you'll end up having more. If you concentrate on what you don't have, you will never, ever have enough."
—Oprah Winfrey

So what amount of money is enough for you?

When I started writing, I had every intention of writing what amounted to a straight finance manual for women. A sort of useful budget planner and a debt reduction guide. But every time I started to write a practical "how to" section, I seemed to veer off into unexpected territory. I hadn't quite realised how much *less important* money was to me than it had been when I had first set out to get it. So that leads me to the question of what really is enough for you.

As a key part of my research, I asked women this: what knowledge and practical things do you wish you had known before you were let loose with your first bank account, credit card and pay cheque?

I was amazed at the response. People flooded me with suggestions. Ladies let me in on highly personal parts of their lives. Although it's not surprising, it is interesting that the same few themes came up over and over again. One of the major themes was this concept of "enough" money. But no one ever actually put a figure on it. When I asked men, they came up with numbers. They wanted a million, or 20 million. Not a single woman did that.

Do you want "enough", rather than, say, a straight million? If you do, then you are like many other women. Women tend to view money and success in a very different way to men. Ordinary women are, in general, much less concerned about *demonstrations* of wealth than men.

We tend to place greater importance on using money to gain security.

Bizarrely, even though we spend a great deal of money on beauty and fashion, the outward trappings of wealth are generally further down the list for women. We want to really *feel* good, not just look *as if* we feel good. We aren't immune to peer pressure; both men and women need a level of social acceptance. We all suffer from insecurities about how we appear to the outside world, but feeling safe and secure is a big feminine-driver.

Emotional needs between the sexes relating to money do tend to get closer to convergence as we get older, but the inherent differences are still there, up to a point, throughout our lives. Almost all of the women I asked during my research seemed to be looking for this slightly-lower-octane brand of financial success. A success measured largely by feelings of security and certainty.

When asked how much money they want, men tend to give a number, and most women give an emotion and an "enough" response. Women tend to be more focused than men on the emotions relating to wealth than the trappings of it. Sure, we all like nice clothes and most of us like holidays and great restaurant food, yet things like that hardly got a mention in my research. I was a little surprised at that.

When asked about money, women used words that described emotions, ideas or feelings. My research kept bringing up financial desired outcomes that didn't have numbers attached. Responses were words like comfort, security, happiness, being able to relax, to help their families.

Having enough cash leftover at the end of the month for women to be able treat themselves was usually mentioned, but it was way down the list.

Let's look at "enough". What does it really mean? How much does anyone need? What is your "enough"?

I went from being £60,000 in debt to having pretty much enough money to last a lifetime. And I will be able to stay that way, as long as I stick to my own rules. At the time of writing I have got almost enough. I'm very close to having as much as I need, in financial terms, to last me for as long as I am here. I won't need it after that.

Start considering your own financial goals now. Decide what you want. When we get into Section 2, you will start putting some numbers to your dreams, but for now, just start assessing how much money you think you want. We will get to the detail of getting it later.

Balancing Attitudes and Bank Accounts

"Formal education will make you a living; self-ed-
ucation will make you a fortune."
  —Jim Rohn, author

I s there a relationship between your attitude and your bank balance?
People pay according to attitude. Whether those people are your
boss, the customers of your company or even your family members
paying you with their respect, their love and their loyalty. Whatever the
nature of the pay, you get paid for your attitude. After all, respect and loyalty need to be earned too, and those things are just as hard to earn with a
bad attitude as money.

So how are *your* attitude and bank balance linked?

It's like this: if you do a great job with a bad attitude, it is only a matter
of time before someone else will be able to do the same job with a *better*
attitude. That person is eventually likely to get paid more, get promoted
faster and be more appreciated.

Remember that your attitudes are what *other people can see* about what
goes on in your mind.

Rebecca had an attitude. She was really great at her job. She had an eye for detail, she worked hard, and she understood the technology that she sold for her company down to every detail. But she had just been passed over for promotion, didn't think much of the skills of the people she worked with and she was not happy.

She resented her new boss, Marina. The year before, when Marina first joined the company, she had been in Rebecca's team as one of her subordinates. Though at that time, it was Rebecca who had been the boss, and she had always given Marina the most difficult projects to do. Awkward! She had quickly been transferred somewhere else in the firm and was now back as Rebecca's boss.

It would have been so easy for Marina to retaliate. After all, she suddenly found herself in a position of relative power over Rebecca.

So what did she do? Did she repay the compliment; did she give Rebecca every poison-chalice assignment? She could have very easily set her up to fail. Marina had a sneaking suspicion that Rebecca would have done that to her (and she was probably right).

Rebecca was dreading the coming weeks, because she knew that it could be the time when her career path was about to hit a few bumps. She expected the worst. She convinced herself that Marina was going to be a terrible boss. She was on the defensive and on the look out to be tripped up. But she was lucky.

You see, Marina had a good attitude. She didn't have a chip on her shoulder from the projects Rebecca had given her in the past. She didn't carry resentment around. She didn't bear a grudge. That's why she had been given the promotion in the first place!

She gave Rebecca the next big project that came in that had an almost guaranteed chance of success. A new system installation for one of their best clients, and it was a nice simple job with a high price tag. The technical implementation had been planned by one of the firm's best designers. It was a project that would be very difficult to get wrong. Don't forget, that on a technical level, Rebecca was *really* good at her job. Marina had to keep her busy enough in those first few weeks not to just control her chippy behaviour, but to actually change what Rebecca believed about Marina.

Marina couldn't change her attitude until she could change the beliefs that drove them.

Marina set Rebecca up. She set her up for success. Instead of allowing Rebecca to create her own "self-fulfilling prophecy" by flunking her first big project under her new boss's oversight, Marina did the exact opposite of what Rebecca expected. She gave Rebecca the best possible chance of success with no hidden agenda of revenge for past treatment. Marina wasn't weighed down by a chip; she didn't have to limp from one disaster to look for the next drama.

Marina's first project as team leader, with Rebecca in charge of the detail, was a huge success. The whole team basked in the glow for weeks. Marina made sure that Rebecca got her share of the appreciation, but everyone knew that Marina had set up the success. Everyone liked her as a boss, and everyone wanted her to do well. She didn't disappoint. There ended up being *two* people with a good attitude. Marina did a great job, and Rebecca started to drop the chip. In a few months' time, Rebecca will probably get promoted herself. Marina was a superb manager because as well as getting the job done, she improved someone else's chance of success and demonstrated a good attitude. That's what she got paid for. She got paid for having the attitude of a leader, not just delivering on the project.

Women can be great at taking into account the emotional elements that drive people, because we take time and energy to get them working on our side. We don't all have a perfect attitude all the time—but we can all work on it.

Do you think it was easy for Marina to give Rebecca an easy project, or would you have understood if she had given her a stinker to teach her a lesson? A few years before, Marina probably would have given her the stinker. But she knows better now; that's why she was being paid more. Not because she knew more about IT, but because she made better decisions, had better control over her emotions and managed her attitudes.

So can you educate your attitudes?

Yes, you can. But here's the rub you need to watch for if you don't want to run out of steam when it feels like hard work.

When you make a change, there is often a delay between the time when you create the shift, and when it shows up as a credit. You will certainly get your pay rise, but there can be a big time lag. It can take a fair while for the cash to catch up. So many people give up before they see the reward. So how do you keep a positive attitude for long enough to get wealthy?

One secret to managing the delay for long enough is to expect the delay. Understand now that it takes time to filter through. Forewarned is fore-armed as they say. You will need to know so that you don't get ratty about it and revert to old habits just when the money is about to start flowing in the right direction.

The delayed reaction is one of the key problems. There's a direct comparison to dieting. It's the same problem. When you overeat today, it can be days or even weeks before you really see the behaviour show up on the scales. I believe that it's the gap between the cause and effect that plunges so many people back into bad habits. That bit of chocolate cake may not show up on the scale first thing the next morning, but if you keep doing it every day then it sure will show on your hips over time. It is the same with an attitude that needs adjusting. Changing it for the better won't necessarily show up in your pay packet today, but it almost certainly will six months and six years from now.

Change your thoughts today and you won't suddenly have got rid of the overdraft tomorrow just by thinking about it!

I was having dinner recently with a friend who brought along her friend. I had previously met this other lady but hadn't really got to know her. It didn't take me long to realise that she was far from ordinary. Rachel was a dedicated mum who had an ordinary administrative job in a bank in the HR department. It might have been an ordinary job, but there was nothing ordinary about Rachel. She vibrated with life.

Over dinner, we were chatting about the sort of stuff that you chat about with people you don't know very well: work, hobbies, family, that sort of stuff. She was clearly passionate about both her family and her job. About life in general in fact. She told me that she had been with her employer for a long time. As is normal in big organisations, she told me that there was a program of "re-structuring" going on. That is big company speak for redundancies. Many jobs were being moved to other (cheaper) locations, and the future was a bit up in the air for employees at the bank. There was a lot of uncertainly and fear among the employees at the time, but instead of being fearful of what was going on, Rachel was excited. She had reason to be.

Rachel had always been positive and passionate about her job, and it had obviously been noticed. It was clear that she didn't just *work* in HR. Rachel put the *human* into Human Resources. Here is one tiny example of how she did it. Once a month on pay day, it is normal for the staff wage-slips to be delivered via the internal mail. Not in Rachel's firm. She took it upon herself to do it differently, and had done it her way, for years.

Every month on pay day, she walked to each desk and physically handed over a pay slip envelope to every person in the office individually. It wasn't a small office either; there were more than 100 staff, so each month her walkabout took the best part of a morning. It is not surprising that Rachel knew every single person in that office. She took a brief moment to say hello, catch up, and move on; she took the trouble to speak to everyone. So not only did she know everyone, but everyone knew her, and if my own experience of her was anything to go by, she brightened up everyone's day for a few moments when she was there. People didn't associate her with the less pleasant elements that HR departments sometimes have to administer (like redundancies and disciplinary procedures).

Rachel anchored herself to the pay slips. I am not sure she consciously thought it was particularly clever—she certainly didn't come across that way. There was nothing manipulative about her, and there was no hidden agenda. She simply liked people and cared about them. More than that, she cared about the image of her department.

On pay day, everyone saw Rachel trotting across to their desk with a smile and a sealed envelope in her hand. The details of what was going into their bank account that month always arrived with Rachel. What a fantastic idea. Although it took a few hours to get round everyone, her boss tolerated it. She didn't use the activity to avoid doing other jobs. It wasn't an excuse to take time off the paperwork. Rachel paid attention on her travels. She observed the atmosphere in each department. She wasn't snooping. She was genuinely interested in what was going on with the people and function of the company. She understood which parts of the company were fun to work in and where the staff looked under stress. She probably knew the culture of that office better than anyone. So what happened when the firm re-structured?

Rachel was a part time worker, so she could have been vulnerable. In fact, her job was not under threat. Do you really think they would want to lose someone with an attitude like that? You cannot be serious! Of course not. Rachel was offered the chance to move anywhere she wanted within the firm. She was offered the opportunity to retrain for almost any relevant professional qualification that appealed to her, in any department.

She could take her pick. She got to stay with the company she loved, and she was about to land a refreshing change of direction and more highly paid role.

She would be able to stay part time and still spend the time with her daughter that mattered so much to her. If the company ever leaves her town, or suffers some other terrible fate, she will be better qualified to get another job than ever. She has made her own insurance. There must have been a whole host of technical skills and experience that Rachel brought to her job that I didn't hear about. I am not suggesting that taking the pay slips around the office once a month was the only secret to her success. But it reflects the attitude and enthusiasm that she took to work with her. That is just one element of what made her so good at her job and great to have around.

Rachel's story is a fantastic example of what having a positive attitude, and knowing what you enjoy doing, can deliver. Rachel is a people person, and no matter how much HR departments the world over have a tendency to tie their staff to desks, up to their ears in admin, she wasn't having it that way. She is a gregarious person who went into HR because she liked dealing with humans, not just paper representations of humans. If I had owned a company with staff at the time, I would have employed her on the spot, and doubled her pay! What a smart lady. The bank is lucky to have her, and they know it. Was she better at the other parts of her job? I honestly have no idea, but I can bet that Rachel made her own luck by being the person that everyone was pleased to see. The final bonus was this: because she knew which departments seemed to have the most fun, she was able to make an informed choice about where she wanted to re-train and work longer term.

These small stories of everyday success can easily go unnoticed. They are happening around you all the time. Your own success depends on you developing your own ability to start noticing the amazing little things that are happening in your world.

Rachel is one of the happiest people I have met in a long time. It oozed out of her every pore. I left the dinner table feeling uplifted after a great evening. Rachel was infectious. She was so enthusiastic about her life, she spilled it everywhere. She leaked happy. What do you leak?

To make a serious start on changing your finances for the better, you will need to start managing your mind more proactively than you probably have up until now. You need to create a good attitude. You can decide to make other people enjoy working and interacting with you, like Rachel did. But what if you lack the confidence? What if you sabotage yourself, how do you deal with being your own worst enemy? Let's look at that next.

Give Self-Sabotage a Kicking

"Self-sabotage is when we say we want something
and go about making sure it doesn't happen."
—Alyce P Cornyn-Selby

So it's all very well for people to talk about being positive. It's certainly powerful to read inspiring stories and interesting things about values, beliefs and attitudes. But what is really happening when we get in our own way? What is going on when we self-sabotage?

Have you ever sabotaged your own success?

If it were all so easy, with a little attitude shift, wouldn't we all be millionaires already? Oh, if only life was that simple. The trouble is we are often our own worst enemy. We talk ourselves out of taking the steps needed to change.

Have you ever resisted a change that would probably have been good for you because you were a little scared of the unknown? If you have, realise this: it is not a weakness or a character flaw. It's natural, and everybody does at some point. So how do you stop yourself getting in our own way? There is no doubt that with most people I have ever worked with as a coach, the biggest things stopping them are NOT outside forces. It's themselves.

Sometimes our self-image gets in the way. We can paralyse ourselves thinking that it matters that we are too fat/thin/tall/short/pale/etc./etc./ etc. I think that women suffer from this image issue more than men.

Have you ever known—deep down—that you are perfectly capable of doing something, yet still have doubts that you can do it when someone is watching? That is an example of you being your own worst enemy.

Public speaking is a great illustration for this. If you can speak to a friend in your kitchen—if you can string a sentence together while keeping an open expression and staying vaguely on topic—you can speak in public. The only difference is what goes on in your head. Your imagined fear. Public speaking is one of the most common fears of all. Very few people are confident to do it. Yet those same people talk to people one to one every day and don't give it a second thought.

Public speaking is a great example of when most of the population get in their own way. They sabotage their own chance of success by talking themselves out of the possibility of doing well. So let's look at self-sabotage around money.

Think of your mind like a computer for a moment. If it is programmed to think that money doesn't belong in the system, what is the likely outcome every time some comes along? Why, you spend it of course! It doesn't belong with you. You just have to get rid of it, and if you have made a generalisation about yourself that you are "useless" with money, your subconscious will ensure that you stay true to yourself.

That same belief of money not belonging with you can have an impact on the income side too. If you believe money doesn't belong with you, then you may not ever have any spare money to spend in the first place. You may just drive opportunities away from you. People justify this in all sorts of ways; if I earn more I will pay more tax, or I will just give it to the childminder, etc., etc. The trouble with all these strategies that drive money away before it even gets close is that they have an effect on other people too. They tell the people in the world around you that you aren't that interested. They tell your boss that you don't want the overtime or the promotion. They tell your business partner that you aren't as committed as they are. They tell your customers that there is a limit to your interest in giving them what they want.

Those tiny decisions, driven by your values, beliefs and attitudes, all have an impact. They don't just stop in your head. They change how the world reacts to you.

I was fascinated by a book called *Rich Dad, Poor Dad* when I read it many years ago. In my early life, I had two father figures around. They couldn't have been more different when it came to their attitudes towards money.

One spent his life constantly worried about money. He saved money at every opportunity, and if he did have to buy something, he was always on the lookout for a bargain. The other figure was a great spender. He believed wholeheartedly in his ability to earn as much as he wanted. So he had no problem spending it. He knew he could replace it. Money wasn't a scarce commodity in his world. It was there to be earned, invested and spent.

Both were highly educated men. When I look back, I can see how those attitudes coloured every aspect of how they lived their lives from day to day.

The *saver* always seemed worried about money. It took a heavy toll on his stress levels and on his health. When heating bills came in, we were told to put more clothes on if we were cold. Turning the heating up would be too expensive. We couldn't afford it.

Now, I'm not saying for a moment looking after your money isn't a good thing. It IS a good thing. You need to take care of the security of your future. But when saving money comes to dominate your life, and the worry about losing money becomes a primary driver of your behaviour, it's clear that things are a bit off.

If losing money dominates your thoughts, it is more likely to happen. We all tend to get what we think about the most. What we think about does dictate what happens to us to a large extent and what we end up with. Don't ask me how that works, but I have seen it happen over and over again. It is called a self-fulfilling prophecy. Some call it the law of attraction.

If you spend your life looking for bargains, the irony is that you are actually still looking for ways to spend your money. And even spending on a bargain is still spending! You don't need any financial education to realise that spending less money still involves spending *some*.

Now, the other character in my life had a completely different attitude. Spending money wasn't a goal in itself, and yet it was something that he wasn't frightened of doing. If your own focus is making it, rather than spending it, then what have you really got to fear if you spend some of it along the way? If your belief is that if you do a great job and people will always want what you have to offer, and money will flow to you, how are you likely to project yourself to others? How are you likely to behave differently?

Charity is a good reflection of a healthy attitude towards money. It is almost exactly the opposite to self-sabotage. It demonstrates more than generosity. It demonstrates a self-confidence. It shows that the giver knows what they need for themselves, and how much of it they know they don't really need. It also shows their confidence in being able to replace it if they are giving away life-changing amounts of money.

If you give £10 to a charity dear to your heart, and you are struggling to pay your electricity bill, £10 is a life-changing amount of money! We are not just talking big numbers here. How big the number is only relates to the circumstances of the giver.

It fascinates me that some of the most ardent capitalists in the world give so much of their money away. They have been great at making it. Why should they be frightened to let some of it go?

Look at Bill Gates, Oprah, and Warren Buffett to name a few. Bill Gates has vowed to give away most of the fortune that he built up from Microsoft, and to do it within his lifetime. Warren Buffett is also a great philanthropist. He plans to give billions of dollars away. I believe that those guys are working together on one of the biggest charity projects in history.

All these examples contribute to our beliefs about money. Just remember that your beliefs, however dear they may be to you, are constructs. Your self-image is a construct. It's all in your mind. It can all be used for self-sabotage if you are not on your guard a little.

But what if your internal software causes you to self-sabotage because you believe you aren't worthy of more money? This is where things start to get really interesting.

Unbridle Yourself, Because You're Worth It

"A person's worth is measured by the worth of what he values."
—Marcus Aurelius, Meditations

"**B**ecause you are worth it." It's a great strap line, isn't it? You would have to be on the verge of total despair to believe that you weren't worth the price of a bottle of shampoo, or a tub of face cream. That tag line is artistry in copy writing. It is advertising gold that has brought in millions for the company. It also raises a very interesting question for you.

How much are you worth? *What* are you worth?

On the face of it, these questions may sound a little trivial. At face value, they could even be seen as insulting. But it doesn't make the questions any less valid because they are key to your financial future.

The cosmetic company strap line is so clever because it excludes almost no one. If you have a high sense of self-worth, then of course you are worth it! If you are really low about yourself and are having a crisis about your personal value, then their product is a *treat* for you. The company is telling you that you use their products "because you are worth it", and if you don't use their products, you would feel better if you did. Genius. It certainly makes them feel better; that company turns over about 20 billion euros per year!

There is a great deal of talk these days about self-esteem. I personally believe the rather more old fashioned term of *self-worth* is more useful.

Self-worth is something only you can grant yourself. No amount of money gives it to you. Shampoo doesn't give it to you. A rich husband can't give it to you. No one can. You need to develop it, look after it, nurture it, grow it and invest in it.

If you have self-worth and a clear vision of who you are and what you want, you will be wealthy.

But here is the deal about self-worth. Money does not make you valuable. *You* make *you* valuable. The financial part comes to you when you understand your own value and have the confidence to allow others to see it too. Money does not add value *to* you. **It is a reflection of value.**

Your self-worth, your value, (you have almost certainly worked out already) starts inside your head. Don't wait for others to say it is OK to have it. It isn't theirs to give!

Self-worth can be a fragile thing and can be easily damaged, particularly when we are young. I believe many women start eroding their own sense of self-worth as far back as their school days. There is no way of measuring that treasure from the outside, and because of that, only you know how much you have at any particular moment in time. That makes it really hard for schools to teach you how to have more of it.

If you had a strong academic subject or had a sport you were good at that was played at your school, you will have had an early opportunity to get a taste for success, and build on it from there. But only a select few excel inside such confined parameters. There isn't much room beyond the few who fit the model, and because of that, many really talented and creative people get left out of that experience of an early taste of success. Success at school also has a lot to do with conformity, yet success in the real world has more to do with individuality.

If the subjects that were on your class list didn't fit in with your talent or individual gifts, it would be easy to convince yourself you didn't have any gifts. Thank goodness that the world has, unlike school, an almost endless pot of things that you can be really good at. There are many successful people who actually turned a lack of performance at school or college into a driving force to prove to the teachers how wrong they were.

Not everyone is driven forward by wanting to break out of the pigeon-hole of academic mediocrity. I certainly didn't, and I left school believing I was so bad at maths that I would never be successful in business or any field that was remotely academic. That led me (illogically) to believe, for example, that computers would be beyond me. That self-imposed fallacy was based on the fact that when I was at school, all the computer geeks happened to be the same whizz kids who were great at either maths or physics. It took me *years* to shake that one off. Yet many years later, I ended up running at team of people massively more formally educated than I am at one of the world's biggest computer companies.

I realise now that to be successful either in business or financially has very little to do with maths or pure academic achievement. That was a revelation to me. There are lots of people who are much better at maths than me, people who earn considerably less than I do—and don't manage their money very well either. I only need to look at the household debt statistics to see that! That's not said to show off to you, but to prove that success at school in academic subjects doesn't have as much bearing on your future as you might have imagined.

So what do you think that you aren't very good at, that could in fact, be a wrong assumption based on out of date or shaky evidence? What might your revelation be? What "fact" about yourself might be eroding your self-worth that is just plain wrong?

Schools don't always help much when it comes to learning how to manage your self-worth. They aren't there to teach you the real power over your thoughts either, or your money for that matter... There is scant, if any, attention paid on the curriculum to personal finance. It's a simple fact that teachers, as wonderful as many of them are, happen to be in the business of teaching pupils to pass exams. That is what they get paid to do. They are there to develop young, suitably academically qualified people to become useful employees in an industrialised world. They don't get rewarded by the system for pupils' self-confidence. It is hardly surprising that teachers, who encourage our passion for a subject that they love themselves, are often the ones we remember for the rest of our lives. Sadly, no one has found a mechanism to financially reward the teacher who manages to pass on that gift, but they are remembered by us, and the love for whatever they fired our imaginations with, gets passed on once again.

That is a reward in itself, even if the teacher doesn't always get to see it. It is its own form of wealth: a wealth of knowledge.

Only a small number of teachers have much experience of business or commerce outside academia. The world needs teachers, and they often have an impact on what we consider to be our talents, for decades. They aren't often in the best position to spot the future entrepreneurs and nurture them because that subject isn't on the curriculum of most schools. In addition, hardly any teachers have made a significant amount of wealth outside school—they are too busy teaching, so how could they know (or be expected to know) what it takes to create fortunes and pass that on to us?

The overall point I am making is this. Success at school is not in any way related to success financially or in business. Yet we are almost all programmed into thinking that what we are taught in school is so important. That's not necessarily true.

It's not just that school itself can have a detrimental effect on us either. The other pupils can give us a complex as well. Many people developed their public speaking phobias when they spoke up in class and were sniggered at by their classmates. What I am saying here is this. If you can't imagine yourself with great wealth or becoming a businesswoman, it's not necessarily your fault!

Very few schools are able to provide the wealth of knowledge that is needed to teach you how to manage the emotions that lead to financial success, or to manage your money or make lots of it.

I remember with crystal clarity one day when a careers teacher asked me what I wanted to do when I left school. I came up with a list of things that took my fancy when I was fifteen. I recall that the list included just some of the following: becoming a paleontologist (I thought dinosaurs were cool and figured digging them up would be super cool), a ski instructor (there wasn't much snow in Cheshire but I had enjoyed the school ski trips) and becoming an actress (the school play was a blast). Her reaction was to suggest I go to secretarial college so I could earn a "proper" living until I got married! Seriously.

I think that list was so far outside her realm of experience she was likely just lost for words and said the first seemingly rational or sensible career course that came into her head. I shouldn't be too hard on her. I like to flatter myself and imagine that I may have been chuckled about over dinner that night, or maybe the poor woman was thereafter haunted by her lack of encouragement for a slightly odd pupil. I will never know. The fact of the matter is that her "careers advice" didn't do too much for my dreams, my self-worth at the time or for my desire to see the world and expand my horizons. It didn't stop me from doing one of those things and adding more strange things to the list, but it certainly gave my own self-doubt a nice solid footing for a while. I suppose the poor teacher thought I was a difficult child, prone to fantasy—and she was probably right. Were you *difficult*? Did you have dreams when you were a kid that other people assumed were fantasies when you were serious about them? Maybe you could revive one or two of them and take another look.

I have asked many women about what has held them back over the years, and I have listened to so many tell me that a difficulty of some sort at school or college inhibited their confidence when they went out into the world of work or business. Sometimes just one incident convinced them that they were bad at something and it stuck so powerfully, they never questioned it again.

So often it is the "awkward" ones who do really well later in life. The people who didn't fit at school sometimes get so used to rejection they assume life is just like that. There is no doubt that the ability to deal with rejection and push-backs is a hugely important quality that any successful person needs to develop. Those that deal with rejection well seem to be able to push aside barriers and achieve great things. Those that struggle with knocks from their school days and who don't find ways to break out of the pattern, can suffer from more difficulties later on.

Just remember that the past is just that: the past. You can't change it, but you can always change the future. Everything is still up for grabs for you.

There is so much social pressure for us to conform that it can be hard to be your own person sometimes. Being yourself can be hard, but it is one of the secrets of success in life.

Self-worth is something that you can construct. It is a creation, just like a book or a painting. And like a great work of art, it will never be truly finished. To build it, you need to find the things you are passionate about and work from there. When you are passionate about something, it is easy to become knowledgeable about it—to develop expertise. The world is crying out for expertise. In everything!

Expertise alone doesn't cut it though. The world, even though it is desperate for expertise, is full of experts. There is a defining difference that gives the expertise value, and there is one irresistible combination.

When self-worth and passion meet, no one can resist it.

The Power of Passion

"There is no passion to be found playing small – in settling for
a life that is less than the one you are capable of living."
—Nelson Mandela

P assion. All human beings are attracted to it. Passion starts with the
interests and the thoughts that are only in *your* mind to begin with.
The more fascinated you are about something, almost anything—
from ferrets to physics—the more people will want to share your passion.

That's what music is all about. It's just one example of shared passion.
Music is the sound of emotion. That's why it has such power. The fascinating thing about the development and construction of your self-worth
is that it isn't the subject matter of your passion that is important. Think
about TV for a moment; people enjoy watching all sorts of things on TV
that, in the normal course of their everyday life, don't generally interest
them. But if the subject is presented with enough passion, it attracts millions of viewers.

The Olympic Games is a great example. Millions tune in every time,
and yet the greatest percentage of viewers doesn't play any sport. Even
sports that few pay attention to most of the time suddenly get a new

following. People watch because of the passion, the highs and lows. It is an **emotional** experience for the viewer. Look at a few media personalities who seem widely liked (and who probably aren't short of a bob or two either).

Firstly, the magnetic Professor of Physics, Brian Cox who presents science programmes on the BBC. He is so far from the stereotype of a crusty academic that he caught the attention of the nation when he first started broadcasting. Is the sexy scientist so successful just because he is so clever? He certainly couldn't do his job as a physicist if he wasn't clever; however, there is much more going on than that. There are thousands of professors in the UK alone, and yet very few of them are TV stars as well. The difference is his passion for his subject, and his ability to display it. He truly wants to share his knowledge and he is a great communicator. He makes connections between physics (which most of us don't understand) and things that we can relate to. Even when he has lost me completely on the physics, I'm still glued to the TV in wonder, and so are millions of others. His passion is what he gets paid for.

Is passion a talent?

Of course not, enthusiasm and passion are emotions. It isn't his physics theories that make Brian Cox so successful as a broadcaster, is it? It is his emotion about his subject. You could say the same about Sir David Attenborough. There are specialists in almost every field of wildlife study that probably know more than he does. Does that diminish his value? Of course not. We trust Mr A to do thorough research? Of course. We assume he gets his facts right—but really, who cares! That is not why we are captivated by him. We are captivated because of how he *feels* about what he does. His fascination about the natural world is contagious. He draws us into to his own magical kingdom.

Some of the most successful films of all time aren't loved because the cinematography is amazing or they have a great cast; they are so loved because they unleash strong emotions in us when we watch them. Who can resist the chemistry between Richard Gere and Julia Roberts in the modern Cinderella tale, *Pretty Woman*? The film moves through tears, laughter and passion. The incredible *Forrest Gump*, as well as being incredibly cleverly constructed, is a film about the passion between Forrest and Jenny, love and loyalty to family, and how the seemingly impossible can be possible with passion and determination.

To create films that stay with us, the storyteller and the actors have to be able to make passion believable. When the storyline itself is about the difference between a life without passion and how it can change when you find yours, for me there is no better film than *Jerry Maguire*. If you haven't seen it then let me give you a quick synopsis. The leading man, played by Tom Cruise, has set up his own sports agency and is desperate for clients, money and success. His only client is Rod Tidwell, a football player in the twilight of his career, played brilliantly by Cuba Gooding Jnr. But to Rod Tidwell—it's all about the money. There is a famous scene where Tom Cruise has to show that it's all about the money too.

He has to show Rod that he is prepared to do whatever it takes to get the big bucks for his final playing contract, and in that scene, Jerry is seen screaming down the phone, "Show me the MONEY." It's a humiliating and heartless moment of the film. But here's the rub. Rod has got no passion left for the game. His passion is only for his family.

The turning point is when Jerry summons up the courage to tell the football player how it really is. At home and with his family, he's all heart; when he's on the field it's all about what he didn't get and what doesn't go his way. The agent goes all out to show Rod what's missing from his game, and why he's not getting the contract, respect and adulation he expects. Then, in true movie style it all turns around. Rod rekindles his passion for the game and gets his contract, and Jerry gets his commission and gets the girl too. Although this huge Hollywood movie starts off appearing to be about money, it soon turns into a story about passion, commitment and dedication.

It might be a fantasy story, but the truth is this: all great success takes passion. Passion is contagious, and when you have it, people want a bit of yours to rub off on them. They want to catch a little bit of whatever it is that you have, and they are prepared to pay for that.

We love to watch a passionate performance in the arts, on the sports field, about science or in the classroom. Most of us remember a teacher who truly loved their subject and helped us to find an enthusiasm for something we didn't imagine would fire us up.

Singers and musicians who are able to share their passion for music and access feeling and beauty themselves allow us to share that passion for a little while. We all love passion, and those who can demonstrate it in almost any field, fire our own imaginations.

Gillian Lynne, the woman who choreographed the musicals *Cats* and *The Phantom of the Opera*, is an example of passion. I heard a talk by Sir Ken Robinson who related how she became a dancer and ended up choreographing some of the stage's most successful ever productions. Gillian had a short attention span at school, to the point where she was taken to an educational specialist for a diagnosis of her "difficulties". Luckily, the gentlemen doing the assessment recognised that she needed to move to think, and suggested to her mother that she go to dance school.

Gillian Lynne became a ballerina with the world famous Saddlers Wells Ballet and went on to have her choreography work seen on the stage by millions of people. Sure, she obviously had a talent, but was it her talent alone that made her such a phenomenal success? There are thousands of talented dancers and thousands of choreographers. Why do you think she went on to work with the best in the business? Do you really think that such creativity comes from mechanics or even just pure talent?

The more you pay attention the more you will start to see that it is rarely the exceptional knowledge of a successful person that is the only reason they reached the top. So start to really take notice. Your journey to wealth requires that you pay attention to success. Every time you see a celebrity on TV, or the big boss of the company you work for (if it is a successful company of course), take a closer look. See them through different eyes and see if you can work out what attitudes they have.

If you are just chasing the expertise so you can get the money, you will be chasing the wrong thing. It is the passion that is the biggest ingredient that makes successful people what they are.

Find your passion.

Don't Let Words Hold You Down

"But if thought corrupts language, language can also corrupt thought."
—George Orwell, from the novel 1984

C an the language you use when you talk to yourself, and talk with others, affect your wealth and your happiness?

There has been a great deal of research into this area. Back in the 1970's at the University of California, psychology student Richard Bandler started working with linguistics professor John Grinder.

Together they studied language patterns, behaviour and how they linked together. Bandler had previously studied mathematics and computer science, and so they were looking at human behaviour from some very interesting angles.

That early research developed into the field later called Neuro-Linguistic Programming, or NLP for short. Some people like to call it the science of success. Bandler and Grinder uncovered how our language patterns reflect, shape and drive much of our behaviour. They discovered that, in our quest to make sense of the world, we use generalisations to make sense of complexity.

There are many aspects to NLP. What is relevant here is the linguistics and how they affect your belief system. You already know that you will act consistently with your beliefs, and it's because of that this topic is worth further inspection.

Bandler and Grinder identified a language pattern that they called "complex equivalence". They found it had a strong part to play in the development of our belief systems. Almost anywhere you find strong opinions, you will find complex equivalence language patterns. If you want to develop flexibility that will enhance your life, it will help you to understand their findings.

What they discovered is that we all create links between two unconnected events or statements to reach conclusions. These conclusions then form part of our own model of the world, and we use them to make decisions and to decide how to act in certain situations. When an emotional trigger is also present, these "artificial" links between thoughts can become very strong. The statement that "being rich won't make you happy" is a good example of a complex equivalence. If you make the connection, and then see enough rich people who aren't happy, then that statement moves from a generalisation to a belief. The clear implication of this phrase is not literally that money will not make you happy, but that money *will* make you miserable! While it is clearly true that money in isolation is unlikely to make you happy in every area of your life, it IS true that money will NOT, in itself, make you miserable. The belief that "being rich won't make you happy" is a common one in families that don't have much money!

Whenever we notice something that has the capacity to reinforce the link that we make in our minds, we re-enforce it. As the link strengthens, our constructed belief about that link becomes stronger and stronger. We are not generally that good about gathering evidence to support our views, without doing it from a point of bias. Beliefs are largely a construct. A way for us to make sense of the world. They are not all true.

We all have a natural tendency to re-enforce our own treasured beliefs. It takes a lot more work for you to seek evidence to challenge them than it does to leave them be. But if you want to move on in your life, you probably need to develop some new beliefs and doubtless will need smash some old limiting ones too.

You need to start looking for evidence to challenge your assumptions, to bring into question any beliefs that you have that are holding you back.

Some of the beliefs you have constructed during your life will be about the world around you, and some of them will be about yourself. Every time you catch yourself making a negative generalisation about money (or yourself!), stop your thoughts right there and challenge yourself to find some examples that challenges it and breaks it down.

After a few deliberate interventions on your part, you will affect your own relationship with money. You will become a bit less fixed as a person and more open to new ideas. Over time, more doors will open for you. Challenge those assumptions, knock down those old beliefs and start believing things that are going to help you to be more confident and effective every day, every week and every month. When you start using the power of words both on the inside (in your mind) and on the outside (with other people), you will be amazed at how your life can change for the better. You will also start to learn fascinating things about other people and be able to help them solve problems too. These are both wonderful things—and they can enrich your life more than you might currently be able to imagine.

Mistress or Slave to Happiness?

"People say that money is not the key to happiness, but I always figured if you have enough money, you can have a key made."
—Joan Rivers

How closely linked are money and happiness?

It is an eternal debate. Modern western society and our eco-
nomic-growth obsessed politicians depend on you believing that
money and happiness are firmly linked. It is a link that is embedded in
our society.

Happiness is often portrayed as images of people enjoying their possessions, sipping cocktails on beaches, or living in beautiful houses. In other
words: living the dream. Yet we are constantly told that money doesn't buy
happiness. So which is it?

The link between money and happiness is indeed very strong in western
culture. Our corporations go to great lengths to ever strengthen the link
between the two.

Beyond a certain level of basic requirement, there is a limit on how much
money most of us actually need. Before you build your picture of your

financial future, I will be suggesting later in the book that you put some thought into what you actually want from your money. By that I mean, what you want **beyond** consumer goods and the facility to show other people how successful you are.

Money and happiness DO go together when you have developed as a person and created something that other people recognise as being valuable. In this situation the person with the money has been recognised for a job well done. There is more to it than just the money. The money is only the quantifiable applause. When we are peddled the idea that we can have the dream without doing the work (which is what provides the *real* satisfaction), things can go wrong. That's when the money–happiness link breaks down. The whole idea that money gained without effort (like the lottery) is as much fun as money earned is why people get so confused about the money–happiness relationship.

Consider the nature of most advertising. Take holiday adverts; they are full of smiling faces. The subtext is to get the viewer to strengthen the link between being able to afford to go on holiday with the chance to experience an almost unrealistic level of happiness. It's no accident that consumer complaints are amongst the highest in the holiday industry. Our expectations about how much happiness our holiday money should buy are off the charts bonkers. When things go wrong with that precious time we get dingbat angry or drop into a deflated depression about the pain of the whole holiday experience. It's never a happy outcome when things go wrong; ask any holiday rep.

It is the same with car adverts. The brand builders in the auto industry use every trick in the book; amazing images generate positive emotion, then they show you the car and strengthen the manufactured link. *Their* manufactured link. The clever ad men then add music to the mix to increase your emotions further and deepen the power of the link even more. They do everything they can to build emotion—preferably a positive one in the area of consumer goods—and attach their product to it.

Think of the near orgasmic woman in the old shampoo advert. If you were listening from the other room it sounded like a porn movie!

Emotional and behavioural links are being deliberately created, on our behalf, all around us. It is happening every day. On the sides of buses, on TV, in newspapers and magazines and on every search engine and on millions of websites. Unless you live in a cave, you can't get away from it.

Businesses are always trying to get us to associate the ability to buy things from them, using the construct of happiness.

But what happens when we follow the program? What happens when we accidentally anchor our expectations to *someone else's* concept of being happy? What happens when we anchor our feelings to the images and pre-formed expectations to things that we are *told* should make us happy? The answer is simple. We leave ourselves wide open to disappointment.

No car advert shows what happens when you get into your shiny new car after a row with your other half, or what happens when the roads are closed and you are late picking the kids up from school. They don't show the look of disapproval on the faces of the other parents because you were late, or the telling-off you get from the headmaster. The adverts don't show what happens when the dog is sick on the back seat; I have yet to see a car being advertised as "vomit resistant".

Those things happen in real life but not in the advert for the car. It would break down the relationship between buying their product and being happy. Good for your bank balance, bad for the car dealer.

So how do you deal with the happiness and money link in a way that serves you?

There is no doubt that some things that money can buy do give us the opportunity for some happy times. Just learn to be realistic—and choosy. Yes, a nice car can give you a feeling of comfort and security, but not during a row with your other half. Holidays do allow you to experience new things and meet new people, but they aren't going to give you 24-hour-a-day pleasure. You may still eat a dodgy salad and spend the night feeling sick. There are limits, so set your expectations accordingly. Beware of buying someone else's vision of happiness. Get your own vision, earn the means to get it, and then go buy the bits you are going to really appreciate. Remember, don't buy stuff you don't need to impress people you don't like with money you haven't got.

True happiness is not about getting more "stuff". True happiness is related to feeling confident that you can look after your long term needs. That is a feeling that never goes away. It never breaks down, and it never gives you food poisoning. The satisfaction of knowing that you have pro-vided for yourself and your loved ones is unmatched by any "stuff" I can think of. No car or holiday can do that for you. When you can pay in cash, the car or holiday at least has the chance to fulfil some of the promise that you may have been led to believe it should, and it should be paid for with money you can afford to lose. That way you minimise the possibility of being too disappointed if something goes wrong. You take the pressure off all round. If it goes wrong you can also fix the problem. You can pay a nice man to mend the car, to pay for a private doctor if you or your kids need one, or to upgrade to a hotel that serves safer salad.

There is no doubt that *not* having enough money to live without financial stress does have a negative effect on everyone. Unless you have chosen to become a nun and withdraw from the outside world or unless you choose to totally abdicate from financial responsibility. But that isn't possible for most of us.

We all have bills to pay; we have to get by.

We have to shelter and feed ourselves and provide for our families. Even if you are part of a household where there is another breadwinner, passing over responsibility may eliminate the need to earn money for now, but it doesn't get over the problem of security. It doesn't remove the emotions attached to money worries, even when your household seems to have plenty. What if the breadwinner loses their job or the business folds? What if they fall ill? What if they leave? Handing over responsibility may be a temporary fix to push the worry somewhere else for a bit, but it doesn't get rid of the doubts altogether.

More relationships breakdown because of money troubles than for any other reason. And it is a sad fact that many people live inside relationships they aren't happy in because they can't afford to leave.

Money might not buy happiness completely, but it does buy you choices.

You need to decide for yourself what it is that money can buy for you that you really value. Money buys much more than luxury. It buys the choices of how you spend your time and who you spend time with. It allows you to decide what you can focus your attention on. Having money allows you to pick your interests, hobbies and passions.

To be truly happy, you need one plan for you finances and a parallel plan for your life that runs alongside it. A plan that's not totally focussed on "stuff" that other people want you to buy. It's not about helping strangers to make themselves financially free on **your** credit card.

The biggest news here is that happiness is also a construct. It is, to a large extent, a figment of your imagination. Note that I did say **your** imagination. Not someone else's! That would be falling right back into the realms of consumerism again.

Happiness is a decision. It is something that you create, something that happens in your head. It is **NOT** something that just happens *to* you. You make your own future in just about every sense.

No book about money or personal change would be complete without some mention of goal setting. Goals are just promises that you make to yourself. Goals may sound like a cliché, but you can't avoid them if you really want to get on. Having clear goals helps you to decide which way to turn when you get to a major intersection in your life. You need a clear destination. The last thing you want is to work hard without a clear purpose. You don't want to drive round and round in circles with your foot on the gas without knowing where you are going, and if you don't start with your values, beliefs and attitudes aligned, you can end up taking one wrong turn after another.

When you have alignment, balance and clear promises, previous dilemmas will often melt away and become obvious choices. Forks in the road won't slow you down too much. With good alignment in your life, it is like having a full tank of fuel, a clear view, a known destination and plenty of signs to get you there in reasonable time.

Some places along the road will be outside your current range of experience, and you will find the journey challenging at times. You will need a guide so that you keep wrong turns to a minimum. You will be better off if you can keep to the clearest roads: whichever route you decide to take. Call it Sat-Nav for the mind and soul.

Money and happiness can be linked in the way you want them to be. Struggling for money from one day to the next does create unhappiness, because we all struggle when there is *too much* uncertainty in our lives. And remember this about possessions: don't buy stuff you don't need to impress people you don't like. You will only alienate those around you that you do like, who can't afford to keep up.

Getting Help to Cut the Chains

"It seems to me shallow and arrogant for any man in these times to claim he is completely self-made, that he owes all his success to his own unaided efforts. Many hands and hearts and minds generally contribute to anyone's notable achievements."
—Walt Disney

I have had help and guidance numerous times. I have also felt very alone at times, too. That just seems to go with the territory of really growing up and taking personal responsibility for yourself.

I got a great deal of help from books. They were marvellous companions that provided me with an insight when I didn't have the skills or contacts to get a new perspective from anywhere else. There have been many times when I was too scared to admit how much I didn't know, so they saved me from much embarrassment.

Everyone who achieves great things has help sometimes. No one can make the move from a bad place to a good place totally on their own. Your companion may be a book, a partner, a husband, your family or a friend. It is most likely a combination of different people who will be helpful at different times for different things. Prepare to be open to having help, whatever form it takes.

If you are genuinely isolated because of your location or circumstances, there is a massive support network out there, ready to welcome you online. There are thousands of internet groups that can be the basis of a support network to get you started. No one faces total isolation any more, unless they choose to. Whatever your experience to date, have faith in the knowledge that there are many people out there who face similar challenges. For example, I am someone who is a compulsive sharer of good stuff. I can't help myself. It is part of my purpose and a good deal of my passion. If something out there is great, and helps me, I want as many people as possible to know about it so that they can benefit from it too. That keeps me aligned. It is a big part of who I am. That keeps me connected to people, and it ensures that I don't exist in isolation. You will be finding your purpose, your alignment, and those things will help you to connect with others. That connection is part of what makes people happy. Without connection, you can't make money either; because if you can't add value to people's lives, why *should* they share their hard earned money with you for a service or a product?

Accept help wherever you can find it. You also have great capacity to help others in their own search for wealth, too. Helping others see the best in themselves can sometimes be enough. Try and surround yourself with people who enjoy seeing your success, and find ways to meet people who have already done what you want to do. You will be surprised how much help they will offer to someone who is excited about their own future and has a genuine desire to learn.

Get help!

Are You Ready?

"Talent alone won't make you a success. Neither will being in the right place at the right time, unless you are ready. The most important question is: 'Are you ready?'"
—Jonny Carson

How long will it take you to be ready to move along the path to financial freedom?

The answer will be different for everyone, and only you can know when you are ready to get started. Many authors and coaches advocate taking instant action. Not only that, you must take it right now! You should never leave the moment of a decision without taking action! I don't disagree with the concept; it's just that it doesn't happen very often. Most people have good intentions but don't get round to the action part.

You will delay action whenever the behaviours required would conflict with any of your personal values or beliefs. What is sometimes disguised as lack of motivation or procrastination is, in fact, just unresolved internal conflict.

Looking from the outside, it can appear that women who have gone from crisis to triumph made a monumental breakthrough and never looked back. It can appear that they took instant action—and lots of it. In some ways that is true. But what you need to recognise is that every person who has overcome a difficult obstacle and turned things around did it **when they were ready.** Getting ready can be the hardest part. By reading this, you are getting ready. You see, when you look from the outside, all you see is the action. You will rarely see any of the internal suffering or stress that came before it. Most of us will attempt to hide our suffering from the outside world. No one wants to broadcast their weaknesses. But over time, weaknesses can serve us; they are not something to hide. I know that might sound odd, but I can tell you with the benefit of hindsight that it's true.

The day I had the repo man standing on the doorstep of my flat, I didn't start ringing around my friends and family telling them about my failure. I was ashamed. Now I have overcome the financial challenges in my life, and I am certain that no one can ever take a car away from me. But back then, in the heat of the moment (and for a long period afterwards) I kept it a secret. I felt I had to keep the experience buried deep and hidden from the world.

You will make decisions and changes in your life when you are ready, not when anyone else tells you to. I wouldn't be so arrogant as to tell you that you must change now. Only you can give yourself permission to do that.

But here's the thing about getting ready to make changes that you do need to know: getting ready is an **active process**. It won't just happen. You won't just wake up one day and BE ready. It doesn't work like that.

There is a massive difference between *getting* ready and *being* ready! Getting ready to grow, develop and get the outcomes you want takes time and effort. If you haven't acted yet, you aren't ready yet. It is as simple as that.

You have a unique way of getting yourself ready. Different things drive you; you are not motivated in the same way or by the same things as other people. That means their timelines won't work for you. They won't apply. Only you know when the time is right. Give yourself permission to get ready **in your own time and in your own way**.

If you keep getting ready to make the changes you want for long enough, if you keep putting the effort in, at some point you will BE ready. At that point, when you are ready, you will start to take action. No one else knows what you need to have in place. No one else can tell you when you are ready.

No one else can tell you when you are emotionally fully prepared to take the leap into action. And no one else has a right to tell you to do it on a timetable that would be the same as theirs.

Just for a moment, I want you to think about the last time you went for a big night out. A real treat of a night. It might have been out with the girls or for a special dinner with your other half. Whatever it was, how long did it take you to get ready?

The reason I ask is this. Developing your skills and attitudes so that you are in a position to get wealthy does have some things in common with getting ready for a special night out. Actually getting dressed doesn't take more than a few minutes. Physically putting on the clothes takes just a minute or two. It's the having everything in place and all the preparation that takes the time. And the extra time you need to allow for when you change your mind if your planned outfit doesn't feel right on the night. All women are all really good at planning when it counts. So it is with money, too.

You can no more get wealthy without going through some specific steps than you can go for a night out without putting your clothes on.

There are many different ways to get ready. You can read everything you can get your hands on, you can formally educate yourself, you can mix with new people, you can ignore the bad things and focus on the positive things, you can turn up the pain in your life until it becomes unbearable, or you can let other people (like bailiffs) turn up the pain for you. The brand of getting ready will be your choice. When you are ready, you will take action. And when you feel ready, you will be ready to really commit.

Are you the same person you were last year, five years, or even ten years ago? Almost certainly not. You are changing all the time, even though you might not be aware of it, so you may as well take control of *how* you are changing. Start making conscious choices about your thoughts and actions. From chatting to friends and relatives, it appears that many women don't think about change and development very much. Have you just been changing by trial, error and accident until now?

There is a famous saying: "if you do what you've always done, you'll get what you always got." Change is good. Don't resist it. It brings new possibilities and new outcomes. It brings variety and excitement. Life would be very dull if we always knew what was around the next corner.

It was Oscar Wilde who said that "experience is the name we give to our mistakes". How true that is. We are all programmed to avoid mistakes, and yet it is the mistakes we make that teach us so much. Reducing the fear of making mistakes allows you to make more of them and increase your learning opportunities. So start to pay increasing amounts of attention to choosing what you watch, who you decide to listen to and who you spend time with. You are going to change as your world changes, even if you don't notice. Start changing by design and not by accident.

Ultimately, taking action is the only way to get wealthy. You, and only you, will know when you are ready to start.

The Power of Purpose

"If you follow your WHY, then others will follow you."
—Simon Sinek, Start with Why[2]

Have you ever asked yourself the question of *why* you want more money?

That question isn't as silly as it sounds. If you haven't got any money at the moment, then it might seem obvious why you want it. You don't just want it, you *need* it! You need it to pay your bills, you want some money left over for yourself after you have paid everyone else, and you might long for the luxury of not worrying about it anymore.

Do any of those possible answers ring true for you? Although these sample (and pretty universal) reasons may seem strong to you right now, they aren't strong enough, and this is why. Those reasons just might get you far enough to pay your current bills (eventually) and even a little farther, but if you don't know *why* at a deeper level, they won't take you much farther in the longer term. They certainly won't get you to the point of being genuinely wealthy. Let me explain further because understanding this point alone can change everything for you.

What's likely to happen is this. Soon after you have achieved the point of bills plus a bit left over, you would likely relax your efforts, then run out of money again and be back to square one. You need more money again, the worry and the stress start up once more and the cycle starts all over again. If you are just paying bills—plus a bit of bonus now and then—why would you go through the extra effort of doing more? If you don't have a deeper reason to drive you, it will be really tough, and it will be hard to keep going.

So how can you make it different this time?

The answer is to find your own overpowering reason and let it drive you from the inside. When you know your deeper reasons, your own **"why"**, you work and focus on a different level.

If you are broke, you probably think I'm insane talking about this **"why"** nonsense. You may even think that if I don't know why people need money by now, I should read a few more books myself!

When you haven't got enough, paying bills and surviving seems like the strongest reason in the world, I understand that. What you need is all-consuming, especially if the bailiffs are on their way round to your house. It seems like a good enough reason when the repo man is outside the front door. I also know the cycle of needing money over and over again. But now I know better. Having a shopping list of what you need and want today isn't enough. That's one of the reasons I wrote this book, to help other women break free of the riptide and swim to the safety of financial freedom once and for all. Here are the reasons why just having a shopping list for things you want to do with money doesn't work.

Firstly, not having any money, enough money, or wanting more money is just not **specific** enough. The second is that it's not **motivational** enough. The third reason is that just needing money doesn't allow you to think **beyond** the problem. And you do need to find a way to think *beyond* the problem.

If you don't, even if you have managed to motivate yourself to solve it this time round, you are likely to get sucked back down by the riptide all over again. That's because you never get far enough out of it to swim free. Your reason has to be your infinite energy source, AND you have to be able to think beyond the problem. Motivation doesn't do the trick on its own. It's not enough.

Motivation comes from your **"why"**. Motivation IS your **"why"**.

So let's look at the "why do you want it" question in more detail.

Motivation – Your Infinite Energy Source

"A man always has two reasons for doing anything: a good reason and the real reason."
   —J.P. Morgan

Do you have a powerful reason for wanting the money that goes **beyond** paying the bills and having a bit leftover?

If you don't have a big reason to do what it takes to get the money that you want, you are likely to take the path of least resistance and get sucked back underwater when the going gets tough. You need a bigger reason to go through the effort required to become free.

A good start is to remember that you are doing all this to improve your whole life; you are not doing it for money for its own sake. The truly wealthy don't push themselves to the limits just for the money. Only the masses work for just the money.

I am financially secure, but I didn't get here by working hard to pay my bills. I knew I needed to pay them of course; I had to keep warm, I needed to eat, yet I was constantly being pulled under. Those reasons, however important they were at the time, didn't get me out of bed in the morning easily. I always wanted more time in bed! I didn't truly succeed until I had a bigger reason, because until I found it, I took the path of least resistance and took a rest from it all when I got my head above water. I convinced myself that I was just recharging my batteries but I wasn't. I was just taking time off because it was easier that way.

After all, why would I get out of bed for the electricity company? Why would I want to slave away for them after I have earned enough to light the house? They don't even know me, but the blighters send me a bill four times a year. Although paying the bill was essential, it didn't inspire me. I resented the bill. The price of electricity was just a pain and I complained about it. I have never been excited about paying a bill. Relieved, yes. Excited, no. Electricity, or any other essential bill of daily life, does not give me a big enough reason to work twelve hours a day. Have you ever leapt out of bed in excitement shouting, "Car Tax, I am just SO excited about paying for the Car Tax!"

I often work twelve hours a day or more these days. But I only do it because I *want* to; I **never** *have* to. Because work isn't really work anymore. I do it because I love it. I have a strong purpose. I know my **"why"**. My **"why"** is that I want to play my part, however small, to help women find financial freedom. I have seen too many friends and relatives get pulled under by their own finances, and so much of it could have been prevented if they had been in possession of better information.

I have my reasons. I have my **"why"**. Now I want to do my best to help you uncover yours. So many "how to" books on money don't help because they only deal with the what-to-do part, and not the WHY-you-do-it part.

If you *just* want the money, you are still thinking about trying to control the world outside yourself. That never works long term because you can't control the world. To get wealthy, you have to control your world—the one *inside* your head.

If you do really want to be financially independent then your reasons have to be strong enough to take the rough and tumble of the process of getting wealthy. If you don't direct serious effort into clarifying your reasons for wanting the money, you are highly unlikely to get as much as you need, want or expect. Your reasons and your desired outcomes have to be crystal clear. Without clear reasons, you just won't get round to it. They have to be powerful enough that you don't even notice how tired you are when the alarm goes off in the morning. A really powerful reason will even have you awake **before** the alarm goes off.

I remember reading my first book about money, riches and wealth. I also recall feeling a bit let down. I felt as if I had been promised the secrets, and then all the secrets had been held back from me. Years later, I understood; I didn't have a good enough reason back then to see them. They were there, I just couldn't spot them. Over the years my reasons have developed and matured, and now they are stronger than ever.

Getting your head above water might seem like a powerful reason if you are in financial trouble. Life never seems the same again when you have had your own "pack of bacon day". That horrible day, the one that hits you between the eyes. The one that makes you determined not to live so close to the financial edge as a way of life ever again.

People who suffer a great tragedy don't need to think about a good reason, ask anyone with a sick child. Life or death situations bring out a drive and creativity that can make the seemingly impossible possible. People get amazingly resourceful when they have a sick child. They find ways of paying for all manner of treatments and surgery when the chips are down. If only those same people had that level of drive earlier. If only they had found such strength and purpose *before* they had a problem; just imagine how much more secure their lives would have been. Think how much more room there would be in their lives to deal with the crisis itself, instead of worrying about money when there were more important things to focus on. Don't wait for a tragedy to strike before you find your reason. Find it now.

Here is a big secret about a powerful reason. Successful people don't all start with a powerful reason. THEY CREATE ONE. Some of the worlds' most successful businessmen and businesswomen got their own strong dose of motivation because of their own "pack of bacon day". Something pissed them off and they finally had enough. They found a reason and acted on it. "Away-from" motivations are amongst the most powerful reasons of all. You don't always need to want to move towards something better.

If you haven't got your reason already, go to work on it. Think of everything you are desperate to get away from in your life, and that includes all the bad feelings that you would like to ditch for good. Imagine what you could do if you had enough money to do anything you wanted. Visualise how life would be if you had everything you wanted. Visualise it every day. Pretend it is already real. You will be surprised how your thoughts will start to manifest differently. Then, focus on finding your passion. If you haven't got one yet, develop one. These are the first steps to take to create your reason—your own **"why"**. It might be helping people, it might be spreading knowledge, or it might be preventing suffering.

Only you can decide what your purpose is. When you have it, and you develop greater and greater clarity of purpose, you have your infinite energy source. Motivation will find you, when *you* find your ***reason***.

Away from the Dungeon — Towards the Light?

"The purpose of life is a life of purpose."
—Robert Byrne

A ll those years ago when I had no bacon, it wasn't as if I didn't have a dream, but I didn't have a plan. I thought I was motivated. I was certainly prepared to work hard. I was a really hard worker. Because I got up early and worked a 12-hour day (at least), I believed I was motivated.

But I certainly confused hard work with motivation. Do you sometimes confuse hard work with motivation in the way that I did? For many of us, true motivation starts as a result of a personal crisis or because of intense hardship.

For many women, being able to give their children what they need is their reason. For some, it's to prove a point to a parent or a brother or a sister. For others, it is to break free from the excessive control of a husband, partner or family. It might be to remove conflict from life, or to gain recognition or be appreciated.

There are as many unique reasons as there are people, but there are only two fundamentals that are really in operation here—no exceptions—and this is what they are. We are all driven to do things to either move towards something positive or away from something negative. That's it. These two opposites drive every aspect of your behaviour. Think about that for a moment. Everything we do either moves us away from some level of pain or towards pleasure or comfort.

Many decisions we make are a combination of the two. Even the simplest actions, like getting a drink from the fridge or making a cup of tea, are driven by one (or both) of these. You are either thirsty and want to move away from the feeling of being thirsty, or you want to move towards pleasure, the enjoyment of an icy drink on a hot day or the comfort of a soothing brew. When you're buying a new pair of shoes, it's pleasure. Paying your electricity bill, on the other hand, moves you away from the pain of being cut off and sitting in the dark. Just about everything you do is driven by one motivation or the other.

The trouble starts when your toward-and-away motivations are in play at the same time. Then you face a dilemma. Take buying that new pair of shoes. You might be motivated by looking good or feeling great about yourself on that special night out you have planned (towards motivation). You may also have a reason for not buying them, too; your overdraft is starting to get scary, or your friends might think the shoes are so "last year" (away motivation).

Although this is a fairly trivial example, it is the sort dilemma that gets women into all sorts of trouble. Buying things for kids that they can't really afford is a classic dilemma for mums, a situation when these conflicting forces are in full play. Mums want the best for their kids and want them to be happy at Christmas time, but on the other hand, they know that an Xbox isn't much good when the electricity needed to play it gets cut off.

Dilemmas are tricky, but they are part of life. We all need to take difficult decisions sometimes. Making hard choices can be tricky enough for ourselves. But for mums, when it comes to their kids, they can get really torn. You want to keep the kids happy, to give them a dreamy childhood they can look back on with fondness when they are older, and to be a good mum. Mums want to see their kids little faces light up on Christmas Day.

What about the pain of Christmas Day when you can't afford to give them a nice present? People face financial dilemmas every day, and no matter how much money you have, there will always be some in your life. If you accept that now, you will have a healthier outlook and take some pressure off yourself.

You can use your understanding of your pain/pleasure drivers to understand some of your own behaviours. Even to change the behaviours that you don't want.

By recognising your motivations for what they are, you can start to use the pain and pleasure principal to guide you. They are both powerful forces, and when you find yourself in a dilemma, ask yourself which is the force that will help you make the best decision. Is the pain worth it? Is the pleasure worth it? Will pain now bring more pleasure later? How real is the pain versus how you imagine the pain might be?

Understanding these forces can help you to free yourself and allow you to better manage the complexities of your finances and your life.

On the Pleasure of the Struggle

"Problems are not stop signs, they are guidelines."
—Robert H. Schuller

The dream of so many people seems to be wealth without effort, or at least extra effort. They miss the point. Having it is great, I don't deny it, but it was the getting of it that has been the real fun. If you don't want to do what it takes, to put the work in, you are missing the point of wealth. Getting wealthy can be a total blast. I wouldn't have missed the struggle for anything.

Has it been frustrating? Sometimes, yes. Frustrating and maddening to the point of tears when it didn't seem to be going my way. Did it seem like it was never going to happen? At various times, definitely.

During my research I asked some mums if they had experiences bringing up their children that were exhausting, frustrating, with emotional highs and lows beyond comprehension. They all answered yes. Yet not one of them said they would have missed it for the world. When I asked if they would have rather that their kids had gone through some sort of time tunnel and grown up without all the delights and heartache, they told me that I didn't get it. It was all those things that made the whole thing worth doing!

In essence, having a family is about the same thing as getting wealthy. Most of it is routine, there is a great deal of hard work and repetitive action to be done—meals to cook, washing to do and bedrooms to clean. But amongst the day-to-day slog, there are bright spots everywhere. Moments of pride that make your heart sing. Moments of fear and worry that are more intense than you can imagine. Times that every parent tells me are what make the whole experience so intense.

Building wealth has a lot in common. To try to have it without the process of getting it is just the same.

Being given all the money you needed for the rest of your life on a plate without the effort would be like giving you someone else's grown up family and expecting you to know how to enjoy it and what to do with it. It just wouldn't be the same. You wouldn't feel like you had earned it, and you wouldn't feel connected to it. There can be a feeling of guilt that goes with having money you haven't earned too. Guilt is never a fun emotion. It's just not one worth having, so it is far better if you accept the challenge of making and managing your own money, and then you get the benefit without the guilt to boot.

Doing things that way allows you to enjoy the journey as well as the money. That's a double win. You get twice as much to enjoy.

Money without effort wouldn't be that much fun. It's the struggle that makes the end result so satisfying.

When Things Don't Go Your Way

Why is it that some people just seem to repel problems when others attract one problem after another?

We all know someone who seems to have just been born lucky, someone who goes through life Teflon coated. They find things easy, and they bounce back every time. They stay cheerful. Let's be honest, sometimes you just want to see them fall flat. It's not that we are cruel; it just makes us feel a bit better about our own chaos. But how do we make ourselves one of the lucky ones instead?

Being the lucky one and how you handle disappointment is all down to your beliefs. I have a useful belief that helps me to cope, and it is this: everything happens for a purpose and it serves us. It may sound a bit cheesy but it works, and it works on more than one level. First of all, it makes it a little easier to cope with the rubbish that life throws at me (life does that no matter who you are and how much money you have), because I can convince myself that something good will come out of it. I just don't know what that "good" is at the time; I just trust that it will become apparent one day. How many times has it happened to you that something that seemed so dreadful at the time turned out to be the very thing that opened up a new possibility for you?

Every successful person I know has this belief. Another reason it works so well is that it forces you to look beyond the event or the problem that is so distressing from a new perspective. I find myself looking for why it happened. That's not a retrospective *why*, but a future-based *why*. If you do it too, you will start to expect a different reason for the problem—you start to look for the good that is going to come out of it. You actually start to create good out of the problem. Here is an example that happened to me a few years ago when I tried to buy a house. The story illustrates this well.

The house I was trying to buy was a very sweet house, and although it needed a lot of work, I absolutely loved the location on the edge of my dream picture postcard village in England. I was convinced it was going to be perfect, but I could not get the owners to sell it to me, even though it was on the market. It was one of the strangest purchases I have ever tried to make. My (by now) husband and I tried everything; we wrote to the owners and virtually begged them to sell it to us. We phoned the agent every day for weeks and weeks. Nothing worked. We didn't get the house and I was devastated. I thought my belief that "everything that happens, happens for a reason and it serves us" was plain wrong, for the first time ever. I could not imagine any scenario why losing the home of my dreams was going to serve me. Then, less than a year later, the property market crashed. Not long after that a new waste dump was approved just down the road—within sniffing and rodent running distance of the property. We could have lost our entire life savings if we had ploughed them all into that house.

I even know someone who had a terrible accident that landed her in hospital. Now who would have thought much good could come out of a serious injury, but here's the thing: she ended up marrying her emergency doctor and is now one of the happiest people I know.

Everything that happens to us happens for a reason and serves us. I have never had the audacity to question it again.

Here is another story that shows how the awful can end up being awfully good. I recently read a story about a family in the United States who had to sell their lovely house because of a financial crisis. Their children had been at a wonderful private school, which they had to be torn from. They couldn't

109

afford to buy a house in their previous residential area and had to move to another city and rent in a rundown area. They were out of other options.

They couldn't afford to run a car so they had to buy second-hand bikes to get around. They suffered a massive downward lifestyle shift. The family had ended up where they were because they had put off some very difficult decisions. They had been in denial. In the end, they had no choice, so they had to sit down together as a family to decide what they were going to lose and how they were going to live afterwards. They could no-longer afford to buy toys so they had to find ways to amuse the children without spending money, so they started to play more together. They couldn't buy what they wanted in the supermarket so they started to cook more. They cycled everywhere together. The kids got fitter, Mum and Dad got fitter.

It took a while for everyone to adjust, especially the children, but after a year they were a much happier family. They had been forced into reassessing their priorities. Health and happiness became much higher up the list than money. I believe they are now back on the way to building up their financial reserves, but this time they won't put off the hard decisions if income gets shaky. Their "misfortune" certainly served them. The lessons that they learned as a family will last them a lifetime. As a family unit, they are stronger and proud of their joint achievements.

Another technique to use is this. It is the most obvious one of all but the least implemented. I like to call it my Beatles technique. The Beatles technique is so simple. Just "Let It Be".

That's right. Just let the problem be. You can't change the past, but as we said earlier, you can change the future. Teach yourself to stop getting sucked too deeply into the problem, especially yesterday's problem. If you are preoccupied with the problem to the exclusion of everything else, you are at risk of not seeing the solution when it comes round the corner. You may even miss new opportunities as well. I believe this is why some people seem to go from one bit of bad luck to the next. They don't stop thinking about their problems. The drama of it all becomes a habit. They are so busy trying to put the spilt milk back in the bottle that they don't see the next bottle falling from the shelf until it's too late. More milk spilt, more problems, more drama and the cycle goes on and on.

The last technique I use when things don't go my way is this. I call it my **TLC** technique. Try it next time something doesn't go your way.

TLC stands for:

T **timeout.** don't react, even internally, until you have given yourself time to consider your options.

L **list** your options for how you could react. Until you are practiced, you might have to write down a physical list. These days, I can do it in my head in seconds. It just takes practice.

C **choose** your reaction. Decide on the one that does the least amount of damage to your cause, a reaction that allows you to move forward.

Remember this, although you can't choose the problem, you can choose your reaction to it.

Control the things you can, and do the Beatles technique with the rest. You will save yourself a lot of heartache and a good deal of time. Your time and your emotions can be better used choosing to be grateful for what you do have and looking beyond the problem.

How to Become a Luck Magnet

"People always call it luck when you've acted
more sensibly than they have."
—Anne Tyler

Y ou aren't likely to get rich by winning the lottery, but the good
news is that your life isn't a lottery. You have a life already. You have
already won. You **may** win the lottery (even though someone does
win it from time to time, it would be fairly accidental if **you** did), but the
odds are stacked against you. You have a greater probability of being struck
by lightning, dying of food poisoning or falling out of bed and pegging it
than you do of winning. Your chance of winning the lottery on any given
day is roughly 14 million to 1.

The sad thing is that so many people DO pin their dreams on the lottery. They put so much energy into imagining what they would do if they
did win, they seem to lose sight of the possibility that they could earn it
instead. What a shame, and what a waste of perfectly good dreams!

Before we leave the subject of the lottery altogether, imagine for a
moment, that you did win. Imagine you were rich at the drop of hat. Do

you think that you would *stay* rich? Have you already got the financial skills to look after a large amount of money? Not many people have. Would you be happy after the initial shock had worn off? Judging by the experiences of previous lottery winners, it is not necessarily the case. Life might not be as easy, or as much fun, as you might think.

British glazier Mark Gardiner won £11 million. He went public about his fortune and later discussed openly how his lottery win resulted in him losing all his friends. Some of them he had even bought homes for. Mark said, "I think that, whatever your problems are, money just magnifies them." Take it from Mark, he knows what he's talking about.

Luke Pittard from Wales had a better time of it. He won £1.3 million on the National Lottery, but after the obligatory exotic holiday, a wedding and a new home, he got bored and went back to work—at McDonalds. That is where his friends worked, and he missed the teamwork and the camaraderie. Good luck to him. He recognised that there was more to life than to money. Clever young fellow.

You need to **prepare** yourself for large amounts of money. If you try to stay the same person, just with more money, you probably aren't going to get the outcome you expect. Ask Mark Gardiner. Luke Pittard managed it, but I doubt he imagined that he would end up right back where he started when he was dreaming about being a millionaire. At least he had a clear idea of what made him happy. He knew his onions.

The whole point of the journey to wealth is what you make of yourself along the way. At least then, if you do win the lottery as well, you will probably make a good job of managing the money and you will do great things with it. And one of the things you would almost certainly have to do would be to invest a good chunk of it.

Being a savvy investor can achieve great things. Look at the Princes Trust, just one example. Whatever your opinion about the Prince of Wales, there is no doubt that the money invested in his trust has helped thousands of young people. His combination of the money, mentoring, advice and encouragement has launched many entrepreneurs. It is investors who help businesses and social enterprises get started and help grow companies into meaningful organisations. In turn, these entities employ lots of people. You need to become an investor. You might think that is a long way off for you at the moment, but you need to start thinking of yourself as an investor now. Because investment isn't just about the money. It is about time. But before you can invest money, you need to have some. Time is something you have already. Even if you don't have spare time, you will have the same 24 hours in a day that everyone else on the planet has. If you think you don't have time to make your fortune, then time management skills are something you need work on.

Remember Patricia in India? She started off investing tiny amounts of money into making her jams and pickles then she grew her skills and now has investments in her chain of restaurants, in employment programmes and in people all over India. She employs hundreds of people. She makes a good living and provides secure employment for many families. She started small, very small, but she was an investor from the start. Investing is a wonderful thing. Even if you start with cups of coffee and few home-made pickles.

Invest in yourself first, then in your ideas. The rest will follow.

Don't let the image of greedy banks damage the concept of investing. Investment banks weren't *investing* before the last crash; they were gambling, and they got what they deserved. Sadly the pubic had to bail them out. That was not a good outcome for the taxpayer (you and me), but complaining about it won't get you where you want to go. It takes up too much valuable time and emotional energy. Move on. Make your own future; don't wait for someone else to make it for you.

The material rewards of having long term wealth are just the tip of the iceberg. A massive proportion of your happiness will flow from the effort of getting it. Even if you don't end up with a huge fortune (not everyone wants a **huge** fortune), you are likely to feel like a more fulfilled person because of the effort.

If someone had told me that it was not **just** about the money when I started, I would likely have ignored them. I only needed money, and in my "pack of bacon days", I needed it very badly indeed. The part about being happy wouldn't have helped me much. It wasn't time for me to understand. That's a shame, because if I had understood it then, I probably would have made twice as much—in half the time.

Are there likely to be some failures along the way? Of course there are.

Recently I watched an interview with the very handsome British actor Rupert Everett, who was asked if his many failures as an actor had been the reason that he had turned to writing. He responded by observing how his commercial movie failures as an actor had been the "manure" that had fertilised his success in other areas. And one of those areas was his popularity as an author. At the time of writing, Rupert Everett's acting career was taking off once again. Ironic really. He admitted that coming out as gay had been a career disaster (he pointed out that it would be difficult for him to play the role of a male romantic lead after that), but he was a much happier person for having done it. He didn't have to live a lie. Everything happens for a reason and it serves us. He clearly believed that his failure (as the journalist politely put it) was just food for his next success.

Become your own luck magnet. Make your own luck, and don't wait for life to give you your luck. It's not much more likely to happen to you than winning the lottery.

Getting Your Priorities Right

"The key is not to prioritize what's on your schedule, but to schedule your priorities."
  —Stephen Covey

We all like to think we have a lot of time and that things can wait until you have more time, or more energy or more favourable conditions. But what if you didn't have any of those? How would you prioritise then?

If you knew you had limited time left, you would soon work out what was important to you. The last thing you would want to worry about was being able to pay your bills—or leave others in debt because you didn't. I want to share the story of a dear friend of mine. It serves to remind us of how precious life is and to know what is really important, financially and in other areas of your life.

My close friend Fiona was diagnosed with terminal cancer. Ever the optimist, Fiona was determined to use the time that she had left wisely and have massive amounts of fun with the time she had left. One clear goal was to stay solvent enough to have some fun with those that she loved. The other was to help her sons develop their careers so that they would be OK when she was no longer there to help them.

She talked at length about her priorities and about her wishes for the time that she had left. I remember how she giggled and sparkled as she talked about getting every drop of fun out of every day. She found it liberating that she could drink lager with impunity, eat whatever she wanted—she didn't have to worry about the long term health implications. Talk about managing your mindset. Amazing.

She did need money to do some of the things that she wanted to do with her time. She wanted to go and share some crazy time with her boys, going adventuring in New Zealand. She rafted white-water, threw herself off bridges and saw breathtaking sites.

Although it was clear that money wasn't the most important thing in her life, she recognised it as a great enabler. In addition, she told me that just because she was sick, companies didn't give her free utilities and food, so she had to keep up the good work. We can all learn from such a determined lady. She wanted to leave behind a home as some security for her family. The anticipated few months' survival diagnosis turned into years. Sadly, she finally lost her battle with cancer in 2012.

On the day of her funeral, the gathering was huge. It was the single biggest private ceremony I have ever witnessed. People from many walks of life gathered, and the hundreds that turned up struggled to find standing room for the service. Her sons spoke about her tenacity, enthusiasm and the example she had set to them. (What greater legacy is there than that?) Her husband talked of her unswerving determination, her love, loyalty and total commitment—all worn on her sleeve—and how she had an outrageously good time doing it all. I could hardly believe how one tiny, self-deprecating ball of energy had managed to bounce her way into so many people's lives. As those who had never met each other before started swapping stories, it became apparent just how many she had touched.

Everyone I listened to had a story that was deeply moving. I thought I knew her well, but I was still amazed at how much she had packed into her life, and with so many people. It was like there were about three of her, all running parallel lives. She was a mother, swimmer, athlete, businesswoman, IT expert, she spoke several languages, and she was a coach, friend, confidant, public speaker and a fantastic people manager. The parents of kids she coached at the pool talked of her support and total belief in their children.

Her social friends talked of the life and soul that she brought to every gathering. And there were a lot of them!

Everyone seemed to have a story about how much she liked her wine and beer (often at the same time), and she could drink most men under the table. There were tales of delight told all day, stories of holidays taken and late nights out screaming with laughter. Fiona squeezed every drop out of life—and poured it over anyone who got within 50 paces.

She was one of the most passionate and infectious people I have ever had the delight to share time with. Was she rich? I can't imagine any greater wealth than the aura she carried around with her and that she reflected into the lives of others. Financially she always seemed to get along. She had studied, listened and modelled others who were in her field. She had eventually become a global expert in her own right. So she had worked her way up over the years inside a handful of companies and earned a good living. She relished her final years, even knowing that time was not on her side. She worked from home, almost right until the end. Her boss had no idea how sick she was, such was her capacity for producing amazing work.

She made sure her family was covered with a roof over their heads. She took holidays with her sons, she visited friends and family—sometimes at considerable expense (she had friends all over the world and flew to see many of them). She did enough financially to make sure she followed so many of her dreams. Her work was just one of the ways she got the intellectual stimulation her mind craved. She had become successful in so many areas on a grand scale.

She ensured that she added value every time she set foot into a room, picked up the phone or typed a project plan. She had self-discipline and time management skills that left those around her stunned by her capacity to get things done.

She paid her finances enough attention to ensure that she could do what she needed to do. She knew what she wanted and devoted herself to getting it. And she did create what she wanted: adoring and self-reliant sons, a relationship with someone who loved her totally and supported her to the very end. She had a host of energetic and caring people who loved spending time with her. Her competence in her career meant that she wasn't plagued by financial worries to the point where she couldn't enjoy the other good things in life. She never stopped giving of herself. She also knew the importance of paying her bills and looking after those that mattered to her. It allowed her to relish her life. And a large part of what she did was to make sure that those around her had the skills to stand on their own two feet.

She did that in large measure by setting an example, by going there first. Riches and wealth come in many forms.

I learned so many lessons from the time we spent together: how to make the best of every situation and see the best in people. I know that her spirit still has the capacity to inspire other women, and I think that she would be proud that I documented it. Fiona documented everything of importance. It is important that other women know that it is possible to be a wife, mother and a friend—and at the same time be a high achiever with global professional reach and respect.

During her illness, so many people (me included) tried in vain to get her to slow down, but it was not what she wanted. Being productive made her happy. Her professional achievements were an important part of who she was. She was always hungry for information on finances, and we spent time sharing many ideas. We never did write a book together, although we did talk about it. We were both writers by trade after all.

Over the years that we were friends, she taught me by example that what you get out of life is a pure reflection of what you put in. And that time spent being true to your values and living the best life you can is NEVER wasted. I believe she would have built up significant financial wealth too, had she had enough time. She was a millionaire waiting to happen. But the main lesson she taught me was to relish every challenge and to give your all.

Fiona fell into the group of the genetically unlucky. She had to face the fact that she was highly unlikely to make it to pension age. All the women on her mother's side of the family had been predisposed to breast cancer, and she also had inherited the gene that was to ultimately seal her fate. She faced the questions about what was important to her for real.

Most of us go through our lives assuming that we have got all the time that we need. Imagine being faced with the knowledge that it wasn't the case. How would that change your priorities?

Wield Power Over Decisions

"It's much easier for me to make major life, multi-million dollar decisions, than it is to decide on a carpet for my front porch. That's the truth."
—Oprah Winfrey

I f you're faced with a tricky decision, it can seem impossible to know which way to turn. We all have strategies that we have developed to help us make decisions. Very often, we learned these strategies when we were very small. It can be the case that strategies you learned when you were a child, the ones that worked to get you what you wanted, are still the ones that you use now. You probably don't even think about **how** you make decisions.

How you make decisions is worth some exploration. Sometimes it's not the decisions themselves that are faulty, it's the fact that the way you make them no longer fits in with what you want to achieve. If you want to become wealthy, you need to have some great decision making strategies, because you are going to be making a lot of decisions.

We have all seen kids holding their parents to ransom in a supermarket. Some people carry that strategy with them forever. They never grow up.

You must know at least one person that gets what they want using some form of emotional blackmail. Most of us are tempted to use that one in some form every now and then. But there are better ways!

I know it seems ridiculous to suggest if we don't get what we want as adults that we may burst into tears and expect somebody to throw what we want at us. But it is amazing how various influencing strategies that we learned as children do carry forward into our later lives. Our decision-making processes are also coloured by the success or failure of how we have made decisions in the past. There are some great books out there on decision making, so if this is an area you struggle with I suggest you go and read up on the subject. In the meantime, I do have a few tips.

If you have a difficult decision to make, you are not likely to be at your most effective if you are under too much pressure. Try to take yourself out of the loop, even if it's only for a short time. Get some distance. Take a nap, go for a swim, anything to break the cycle of pressure. Let your subconscious do some extra work. It's amazing how solutions can sometimes just pop up out of nowhere when you stop looking for them. If you don't create some space, you can end up making one catastrophic choice after another.

It happens to workers in the financial markets all the time. They make a few bad investment decisions, and then every decision they make thereafter seems to go horribly wrong. In the financial markets, they call it "burn out". In sport, it's often called the "yips". Golfers get it, darts players get it. The "yips" is the polar opposite of being "in the zone." If you're in financial difficulty, your decision making process may well have been suffering from a case of the yips for a while. It can be a highly destructive state when it comes to money.

Thinking about all the good things in your life and the things that you are blessed with will lead you to make better quality decisions. Simply making a written list of all the things that you love before you make an important decision is likely to help you do a better job. You can also use your new understanding of the towards and away motivations to add to your decision making process too. Put your motivations on paper. It will give you more clarity about what is most important to you about the outcome. Lists are so powerful because they allow you to you think about the good things when times are tough. Writing down what you do have, rather than just focussing on what you don't have, can make you feel better instantly. Things look very different when you actually get them out of your head.

So if you struggle with decisions, make lists! List what will happen if you do something and what will happen if you don't. The answer will become easier and easier to see the bigger your list gets. Just keep chopping out the things that are less important to you until you get to the core of the dilemma. I love the strapline of a software company that relates beautifully to this: workflowy.com says, "Make Lists, Not War".

There is another element to you wielding power over your decisions, and that is the speed at which you make them. There is more than one way of defining a good outcome to a decision. One way to look at things is to imagine you want to get every decision right. Personally, I have a bit of a problem with this one because I know that however long I take to make my own decisions, I know for sure that not every decision will be a good one. By accepting from the outset that not every decision you make will be a good one gives you an element of freedom. You can use that reality to not necessarily just make better decisions, but to make faster ones. The reason that's important is this; the ability to make quick decisions almost forces you to make more of them. That's a good thing by the way!

Making decisions is like any other skill. The more you practice the better you get at doing it. Making quick decisions in the full knowledge that not every one of them is going to be right (you already know that, so why fight yourself in an attempt to achieve the impossible), allows you to make your decisions more quickly. After all, the faster you get, the faster you can make a different one to put yourself back on track if your previous one was the wrong one. Every successful entrepreneur makes quick decisions and makes a lot of them. They aren't frightened of making a wrong choice, because they know that sometimes any choice will be a wrong choice. Not making a choice at all is not an option for successful people. You can make a fast decision to turn around if you find out quickly that you are going in the wrong direction.

The longer you took to make the decision, the more likely it is that you will be attached to the decision itself rather than the outcome. Take note of one thing though; making quick decisions is not the same as making *rash* decisions.

Rash decisions are the ones that are made in the heat of the moment. They are most likely to happen when a decision that should have been made earlier wasn't made at all. At some point, usually when people are forced to act, a rash decision is made simply because there isn't time to do anything else. That is not a great way to go about any important decision. The earlier you act, the earlier you can correct your course if you turned out to be wrong. Everyone makes wrong decisions from time to time. Don't beat yourself up if you do, just make an alternative one as quickly as you can. It is a quality that is common to most successful entrepreneurs, so take a leaf out of their book. It will serve you well.

There is a decision process that's right for you. Personally, lists help me, and they may well be a great tool for you, especially while you are developing your own. Use them and see how you get on. Over time you will find a system that you own, one that becomes part of who you are and how you do things. Those personal systems are always the best ones—provided they have been deliberately obtained, not accidentally picked up in the absence of something better.

So to master the art of making good decisions, ones that will affect your wealth and your happiness, and learn to make quick decisions (without being rash of course) and build a decision making system of your own. Add in a preparedness to accept the fact you will be wrong sometimes and the knowledge that you can make a new decision to adjust your course, and you will start to move much faster in the direction that is right for you.

Get a process, get clarity and add speed. That knowledge alone is gold dust. Lists are for more than shopping; they work for decision making, too.

Surrender Some Control to Eclipse Fear

"God, Grant me the serenity to accept the things I cannot change, courage to change the things I can and the wisdom to know the difference."
—Reinhold Neibuhr

There are always going to be things in life that, however hard you try, you can't control. Let's face it: if you could control everything, life would be totally predictable and very boring indeed.

You can't control the world stock markets, saving rates, house prices, pension policy returns or the cost of electricity. You can't personally control every aspect of the business or company that you work for. If you have your own business, you can't control every employee or the actions of every customer. So stop worrying about those things—you can't control them.

But you *can* control your own education. You can control the impression that you leave on other people. You can control how you look and sound to other people. You can control your attitude. You can control how you manage your time. You can control your own decisions about spending money, especially money that is not really yours.

Try listing all the things you *can* control. You will be surprised at how many things are under your direct control. Things that you can do something about. That is where your energy needs to go.

You will never be in control of everything in the world around you. That's just how life is. So don't wait; take control of the things that you can, and start right now. Things will never be perfect. Getting into the habit of recognising the things that you can and can't control allows you to focus on the things that are in your power to change.

The Power of Money as a Force for Good

"Power does not consist in striking with force or
with frequency, but in striking true."
— Honore De Balzac, Physiology of Marriage

I believe that money gives you tremendous power.

Do you remember the late Anita Roddick? Anita founded The Body Shop. From one little shop in Brighton, she created a global brand that really stands for something.

She was an amazing woman who wanted to be able to buy beauty products herself that hadn't been tested on animals. She changed the world with The Body Shop and did a huge amount of good for her chosen charities, for faraway communities, for animal welfare and for her family. She really kicked off the publicity around the ethical sourcing of products and was the spiritual founder of the fair-trade movement.

Did you know that it was profits from The Body Shop that provided the funding for the *Big Issue* magazine. It was one of the first major social projects that Anita's husband (and business partner) Gordon got involved with. Gordon, together with John Bird, created a social project that has helped thousands of homeless people to make a legitimate income. The *Big Issue* has projects on four continents—amazing. It is just one of the many ethical causes kicked off by the Roddick family, and they did it one tub of face cream at a time.

Anita was a wonderful example of what women can do when they have a passion, stay true to what they believe in, and play by their own rules. Anita used her power with great wisdom and confidence. So can you. Just imagine how much harmony you could bring to your own life, and those around you, if you had the power to help them.

Remember that the good Samaritan didn't just have good intentions; he had the money to enact them as well. The true power of money is paved with good intent, and it is up to you to choose to walk down the right path when you have it.

Whip Up Some Intensity and Feel Great

"Class is an aura of confidence that is being sure without being cocky. Class has nothing to do with money. Class never runs scared. It is self-discipline and self-knowledge. It's the sure-foot-edness that comes with having proved you can meet life."
—Ann Landers

Do you anticipate that with enough money you will feel happier, be able to spend time doing the things you enjoy, and be able to relax about your future? You are right, up to a point. You can feel better *before* you have reached your financial targets. After all, how you feel is a choice. Yes, that's right, it is a choice.

That concept was a revelation to me when I first read about it. It seems obvious to me now, but I have been practicing that choice for a long time already. But when I first read it, I hadn't previously thought about it that way. I thought feeling happy was something that just happened when "things" got better. I hadn't twigged at that point that the "thing" that needed to get better was the way I managed my thoughts as well as my money!

Have you ever tried to be at your most effective when you feel bad? Do you make your best financial or spending decisions when life is in the pits? It might take some effort and imagination to feel good if your current situation is difficult, but it is up to you to make the decision about how you feel. Only you can do that.

There are a few things that can help. Distance yourself from people who won't let you feel better about yourself. If that's not possible today, then make a plan to get yourself away from those people as soon as you can. Even just making a plan will likely make you feel better while you are putting up with the crap they throw at you. It will give you a sense of control over your situation, and that will help you to feel better.

Sadly there are people in this world who think that they will feel better by making you feel worse. They may (or may not) do it consciously or deliberately, but their reasons don't matter. Just get away as fast as you can. Don't waste your time analysing their motivations. It won't change them.

What would your life be like if you made yourself a promise not spend a moment more time than you have to with people that make you feel bad?

In a perfect world, we would all like to spend our time with those we love and who enhance our happiness. I'm not totally daft though, I accept that we don't live in a perfect world. But what if you were to make it a lifelong project to spend an increasing proportion of your time with people who allowed you to feel great? Do you believe that this would give you a better chance of generating the wealth you want too?

It took me far too long to understand that I wouldn't get wealthier until I was able to master how I felt, and that part of that came from being with people that helped me to do that. If you have people in your life that aren't helping you feel good, make a plan to replace them with some more positive influences.

A few years ago, I learnt one of the most expensive lessons in my life about choosing the right people to work with. I learned the hard way about making sure that my values and behaviours were aligned well too. I had taken a new job. I was a recruitment consultant at the time, and I had been really happy in my previous job and had performed well enough to delight both my employers and myself. I had loved going into work (I had amazed myself on that one!), and I was starting to make real headway towards paying off my mountain of debt. Sadly, the company I had worked for was sold, and the new owners had decided to relocate my job to an office that was out of reach.

I was faced with a choice. Either move house or move job. Finances didn't allow the house move, so a new job it had to be. I sailed into a new job. The interview process was complete, a formal offer was made, all the formalities were sorted and my first day arrived in a flash.

I walked into the office on a Monday morning and went through the usual niceties of being shown around the building and introduced to the new team. I noticed straightaway that the atmosphere seemed a bit odd; I sensed a tension in the air as I walked through the room. I convinced myself it was my imagination. It was a big open-plan floor filled with about 100 people, all with phones glued to their ears and keyboards clacking away. I assumed it was just the unfamiliarity, combined with being the new kid on the block that I was picking up on. Call it women's intuition (which is a gift I really believe ladies have in bucket loads when we trust ourselves), but things just didn't feel right. I probably should have walked out there and then, but I didn't.

This job was also my first foray into management in an office environment. I was going to be managing four people, and I was duly introduced to my eager-looking team. They were all men in their twenties. Nice, friendly guys in sharp suits with an eager glint in their eyes. There was a clear chain of command in the business, which was one of the reasons I had taken the job, and I had arrived with an excellent track record so didn't think I had much to worry about. How wrong I turned out to be. Now, move forward in time by a month.

I had started to develop a more frequent uneasy feeling on the drive into work. I had seen other people closing deals that were enormously profitable to the company (and to the salesmen). But I didn't like one bit that the celebrations seemed to revolve around how much they had "squeezed" from their client.

Their attitude to sales was meant to be rubbing off on me apparently, but I was resisting, I was told. I was taken to one side and told by the big cheese that I lacked aggression and hunger. Some women can do aggression, but I'm not one of them. The most effective women that I have ever worked with have been great collaborators, some great leaders, but not one aggressive female I have met has brought people willingly along for the ride.

I had a team to lead, and I wanted to lead them, not break their balls.

There was one man in the office that was held up as a shining light that I was encouraged to emulate. A few times each week he would put on a hat, run to the front of the room and ring a bell. Now, I'm all for celebrating success, but on finding out more, I started to get deeply uneasy.

This guy proudly kept a Dick Turpin type tricorn hat under his desk. When he did a deal, on went the hat and up he went to the front of the room, rang the ship's bell and 100 people burst into applause. After the first time it happened, it was explained to me that he didn't do it for every deal. No one would have been able to do any work if 100 people made that much fuss about every deal. The hat only went on when an *amazing* deal had been done. If the profit margin was over 40%, the hat came out. "Why the hat?" I asked. This guy explained that he had just performed daylight robbery on one of his customers. Time to celebrate!

It was the second time I should have walked out, but once again, I didn't. I wasn't a quitter, but I was starting to feel bad about myself just being there. It didn't take long to realise that this company was struggling. They were a big name in the business, but they weren't doing well. The atmosphere that I felt the day I arrived was because the quarterly profit figures had come in, and they were swimming against the tide. Everyone was under pressure. The management wasn't happy, and they made sure that the workforce knew about it.

This firm had built its business in good economic times, when there were more projects than there were people to staff them. Recruitment was easy when they had started. To make a lot of money, all they had to do was to show up for work. Their "Dick Turpin" strategy had worked for them then, but they hadn't changed it when a recession hit. And it was showing in the sales figures. They were taking on people (including me), who had great client relationships, and then expecting them to treat their valued clients in the same way. After all, that was all they knew. It was how they were trained and most of the staff had joined at the height of a boom time. I just couldn't do it. I felt awful. I couldn't look my valued customers in the eye.

I was given pep talk after pep talk telling me that we were in business to make money and that I spent too much time talking socially to my customers and candidates. I needed to watch and learn from Mr Highwayman! Unfortunately, Mr Highwayman was my boss. He had control over my team members. I had been given every struggling member of staff to see if I had what it would take as a manager to turn them around. No wonder they looked eager. They were all eager not to get fired! They weren't keen, they were desperate.

I almost ended up in the asylum. The place and the environment were literally sucking the life out of me. I lost weight, but not in a good way. I was looking gaunt, pale and far too thin (and yes, there is such a thing!). I started smoking again after having a healthy eight years off the fags. I was getting grumpy at home. As is often case with stress, the ill effects crept up on me. I kept trying to believe that the promised financial rewards would come if I stuck it out. I had a mortgage to pay, and I felt as if I had nowhere to turn.

My values about care and attention to my clients, about providing a top notch service and understanding their needs had gone out of the window. I was doing a job where I had to go against everything I stood for. My sales figures plummeted. My team wasn't doing much better. I started thinking that I was useless, that my previous success had been a fluke. I questioned my ability to even function at the most basic level. In short, I started to feel terrible about myself. So what did I do?

I left. It added to the debts that I had just started to get on top of. I had an £8000 joining bonus to pay back to add to the pain. I was also convinced I had let myself down badly. That I had turned into a quitter. I was petrified of the financial impact. I was literally sick with worry. When I handed in my notice, I was told what a disappointment I had been. That they had hired me expecting me to perform as I had in my previous job. That I must have burned out. That "the business" wasn't for me. Nice people, huh?

That experience took me a long time to get over. Never again will I work with people who make me feel uneasy. These days I allow myself to trust my female intuition.

Do you have people in your life who have a way of lowering your mood or who question your competence?

There are as many ways for people to draw you into feeling bad about yourself as there are people to do it. I will NEVER let that happen to me again. I suggest that you don't either. It's not about false pride. It's about keeping your dignity and feeling good enough to be effective in your life.

You don't need to be perfect to get great results. Imperfection is human. Sometimes it can be your biggest asset—when you are comfortable with it.

Some people manage to make a fortune when they embrace their own imperfection. Some great comediennes make it their mainstay to build their material on their own inadequacies or personality flaws. Miranda Hart makes capital form her plain looks, from her height, her clumsiness and how much she was laughed at when she was in school. Joan Rivers builds her jokes on her lack of mothering skills, her age and her extensive plastic surgery. We don't laugh at them, we laugh **with** them.

So, you don't need to be perfect. Perfect would just make you look like a smart-arse, and no one likes a smart-arse. Give yourself permission to stop trying to be perfect. No one will thank you for it anyway. Accepting yourself as imperfect will allow you to tolerate a lack of perfection in others, too. That will make you an even nicer person.

You don't need to be perfect to make money. No one will like you for it, and you will fail on the measure of perfection. You will never be perfect. The best news is that no one else will be either.

Excellence is good enough. Just trust your instincts, work with people who bring out the best in you whenever possible and strive to be the best that you can be—that *will be* good enough.

Financial Stereotyping Unzipped

"Define success on your own terms, achieve it by your
own rules, and build a life you're proud to live."
—Anne Sweeney

Some people still hold a perception about women that our responsibilities as carers should take priority over our personal financial success. Such stereotypes do have an effect on how we live.

In some ways we are programmed to behave in certain ways by society and by our parents and teachers. It can be in their interest that we fit the old model. Most of them do want the best for us and want to show us how we can best fit in—fit in with *their* expectations!

We are so lucky to live in an age where these stereotypes are starting to fade. But there are other issues such as being more successful than your partner. That can be a difficult balancing act. We don't want to use our success to make them feel worse about themselves, and yet it can be difficult if they compare themselves to you. It is possible for your success to make somebody else feel bad. If you have this as an issue in your life, just remember that you are not responsible for somebody else's feelings. Their feelings are just that, *their* feelings, and only they can take control of them.

If the concept of being more successful than your partner bothers you, you could always wait for them to be successful first. You could wait for them to bring the money rolling in for both of you. But what if they can't do it, won't do it or don't want to do it? Then how are you left? You could end up waiting forever. It's just not worth the risk.

What if you are more successful already and your partner is touchy about it? You need to ask yourself what is more important. Your relationship or your ability to stay solvent then move forward into wealth. It is common for one person to wait for the other to do something. If you have that potential situation with a partner, look again at your list of motivations—the things that you desire in your life—then ask yourself if it's worth saving your partner's feelings in order to sacrifice your future.

Maybe they would go on the journey with you, if you asked them to.

Maybe you need to find more creative solutions to make them feel better about working on their projects while you get on with yours. You don't have to be the same for you to be happy together.

Not having enough money to get by is a huge source of conflict in relationships. It is the number one relationship breaker. Dividing an ever dwindling pie just leaves everybody hungry. If you want wealth and security, you do need to be prepared to go there on your own—even within a relationship. You cannot always expect to take everybody with you all the time.

Money and Marriage

"Money may not buy love, but fighting about
it will bankrupt your relationship."
—Michelle Singletary

There is no doubt that financial stress has to be the world's biggest passion-killer.

Married, or not married, straight or gay, whatever the nature of your relationship, there is no greater way of putting a strain on it than fighting about money.

One issue that affects women more than men is this: what happens when the woman is the more financially successful half of the partnership? It is a minefield if it is not pre-agreed and planned. When one partner feels that the other half isn't pulling their weight, it places a terrible strain on *both parties*.

When it comes to money, there are only four options:

OPTION 1 – Responsible Adults Method

You both agree to work together. To manage any differences in earning power ahead of time. To agree on joint financial priorities, responsibilities and plans, then both get on with it in a totally open fashion.

The "Responsible Adults Method" works. Every time.

OPTION 2 – On the Hoof Method

You don't pre-agree on anything. You both muddle along, with each of you roughly contributing what you can when you can.

You expect your partner to do what you do or, at the very least, match it. Then you expect them (as if by magic) to want to spend/save/give at the same rate as you do on the things that *you* consider worth it.

The "On the Hoof Method" works—until one of you doesn't like it.

At some point, your priorities will change or diverge, and someone will be left feeling short changed, put upon or taken advantage of.

OPTION 3 – Oil and Water Method

You don't or can't agree on anything financial so you agree to keep everything separate. You each contribute half to all the joint costs and keep a clear inventory about who owns what and who owes who money. This is all fine while your financials are independent. Oil and Water don't need to mix. But things get shaken up sometimes. What happens if a financial or health disaster hits one of you?

The "Oil and Water Method" only works until there is a problem.

Both parties looking after their own finances only works when you are both working and both earning. As soon as someone stays at home for childcare, or because they aren't working any more (illness, redundancy, or plain old laziness), things have the capacity to go nuclear. It can put the finances into chaos and the relationship into crisis. It is most likely that the two will happen at the same time, and it will double the stress and the impact. One of you will come off worse.

OPTION 4 – Ostrich Method

You can't agree on anything financial so you avoid all discussion around finances and deal with every issue on a case by case basis. You both spend long periods of time ignoring the problem until it is clear that the problem won't go away. It is a constant splinter under the skin of your relationship and becomes an unspoken worry for both of you.

The "Ostrich Method" never works long term.

Although it often isn't an option anyone chooses, a lot of people end up there by default. There are only two ways out of it that give you any hope of being financially secure and happy. You either design and agree to move to the Responsible Adult Method, or you can resign yourself to taking full responsibility for your own earning power (or lack of it) and continue with a life of conflict, finger pointing and dis-satisfaction.

The nuclear option is to end the relationship.

If you are currently an ostrich, you need to face the reality that you have some choices to make. If your partner wants to stay in denial about the whole thing, if they don't want to get on board with your financial turn-around and participate fully in it, then you are left with hard choices.

If you don't make some decisions, if you don't discuss the issues then there isn't much anyone can do to help you until you do.

The "Responsible Adult Method" really is the only long term viable option so you may as well do it now. And do it together.

Or you could stay single of course. Up to you. Your choice.

Oppressed or Blessed — How is Money Used on You?

"Beware of snobbery; it is the unwelcome recognition of one's own past failings."
—Cary Grant

How is money used to control you?

Money is used the world over for the acquisition of various forms of power, some subtle and some not so subtle. Some people use money to win influence. Some use it to win control. Some use it to control the behaviour and choices of others. Some use it to manage the emotions of others.

The powers that money can bring, when used unwisely or with negative intent, can have disastrous consequences on other people. When used wisely and with positive intent, that power can also have marvellous positive effects on people and on your relationships. Being aware of the potential power can help you to insure yourself against the possibility of negative impacts on your own relationships.

Maybe someone else's money has had dire consequences for you? Anyone wrestling with family members over wills or inheritance—however small—will know exactly what I am talking about.

Often, we are brought up with the concept of power and money as a normal part of our childhood. When you were a child, did you ever hear anything like this? "If you don't do what you're told, you won't get any pocket money this week", or "Unless you are a good girl, Father Christmas won't bring you any new toys". Those normal interactions between parent and child happen to almost all of us at some point. We don't even think about them when we get older. And yet, they have a profound effect on us.

If you had things like that said to you, were those strategies effective on you? Were they effective in changing *your* behaviour? If they were, there is a possibility that you will refine them yourself for use at a later date. After all, it worked on you!

If you have done it yourself, it doesn't make you a bad person. We are all human. We all use, and refine, strategies that have been effective for us—or *on* us. That is how we learn. Most of the time, we aren't even aware of these things as conscious strategies that drive our own behaviours. They just become part of who we are.

Taken to the extreme, the pocket money scenario can get out of hand. Think of a parent who insists on certain actions by an adult son or daughter and who issues the ultimate financial sanction for noncompliance: being disinherited. It is the final wrestle for power and control. The final insult.

Joan Crawford famously cut two of her adopted children out of her will, and left the other two a tiny proportion of the rest. When asked why, she allegedly said, "They know why". Money obviously had an impact on her family. It happens to thousands of people every year, and not just to the rich and famous. It happens within ordinary families, too.

That story illustrates the power struggles that abound in families and relationships and illustrates the power of money. Although money is used in families to manipulate behaviour all the time, when it becomes the primary weapon of influence, things can get very messy indeed. Recognising that can allow you to break free from the power it has over you. It might even give you another reason to get wealthy.

You also have a duty to make sure that you don't inflict the same scars on other people. Your kids will certainly thank you for it when they get older, too. Such behaviours by others can only have an effect on you *financially* if you need the money. With financial independence, the power that the giver has over the potential recipient fades away.

The need for independence has been a strong motivator for several of the millionaires that I know. They have driven themselves relentlessly so that they can make their own choices in life. Moving away from financial dependence on a controlling parent or boss can be a very strong reason for obtaining wealth. I love the clarity of this quote:

> *"I have a fantastic relationship with money.*
> *I use it to buy my freedom."*
>
> —Gianni Versace

It sums up my point beautifully.

The use of money can be more subtle, too. It can be used to express many different desires or to make up for other perceived weaknesses. It can be used to exert power in a sexual relationship. It can be used in an attempt establish commitment from others. Has it ever been used to establish commitment from you?

If someone is dependent, it can appear that they are committed, right? Couples that win the lottery don't always stay together. They suddenly have enough cash to be able to make a choice! It is easy for a sense of dependence to be mistaken for a real commitment. In cases of those lottery wins, or sudden business success, it was likely that the money was not the only problem that caused the relationship to flounder. It was the relationship itself! Don't be too quick to blame the money.

So how does money affect **your** relationships, and how do others use money to gain power and influence over you at the moment?

Financial dependence happens within families, marriages, life partnerships, jobs and in businesses. In other words, they are a fact of life. When you have enough of your own money, you will end up creating new financial links of your own. Ones that you are in control of. That might be great for you, just realise that they might not be great for other people if you don't manage them responsibly.

When your turn for wealth comes, you can decide in advance to stay above damaging behaviours that have the capacity to hurt those that you love.

It is important for you to appreciate that when there is enough money it is rarely the problem if it causes difficulty within the relationship. It's the **person** with the money that can be the problem! It's the control that is the problem. Money just allows some people to fulfil their own desire for control, influence, manipulation or dominance. Money is just the tool—the real deadly weapon is the person.

I have seen money used as revenge (in bitter relationship breakdowns this can all too often be the case). I have seen money used as punishment.

You need to decide right now, in advance of having all the money you want, what sort of wealthy person you want to be. You have the opportunity to do marvellous things with money, so make a plan now that allows you to move forward knowing that you will do what's right when your time comes.

The Effect of Your Money on Others

"Money isn't everything, but it sure keeps you in touch with your children."
—J Paul Getty

S o how do *you* use *your* money, at this point in your life, to have influence over other people?

And how do you plan to use it in the future, when you have plenty?

Both of these questions deserve your attention. That's because your own happiness will depend on your answers. Having money and being financially independent can be a fantastic force for good. Not just for you, but for others too—if you are kind. Kindness is the key to using money well. Notice that I didn't say generosity. Kindness and generosity are not the same thing.

Creating your financial freedom is an evolutionary process, and throughout that process you have a responsibility for the influence that you have over others. You won't wake up one morning and say to yourself, "Now that I'm rich, I think I will change how I interact with people". It doesn't work like that. What is most likely to happen with your financial independence is this.

Your own financial dependencies gradually will be reduced little by little, until one day, you realise that they have gone away. But here's the thing: when that happens, there is a good chance that other people will now be dependent on you! The tables will be turned. I can assure you, when that hits home, it's a strange feeling.

A big part of growing and developing is to learn to treat others in a positive way. That is real power, and power of the best kind. In fact, you probably won't get wealthy if you don't. That is power that money can't buy. It is a power that is inside you already. It is the power to be kind. To really *enjoy* your money, you will discover that kindness is the key. The spirit in which you possess and use money will dictate how happy you will be when you have it.

We have joint financial responsibilities within partnerships and marriages. We have personal and financial relationships woven with our families and our children. You just can't get away from the fact, whether you like it or not, that money and personal relationships are tied together to an extent. That is just how it is. To maintain healthy relationships once you have money, it is wise for you to recognise that there may well be temptation to use it to get your own way from time to time. Some people, wealthy or not, indulge in negative behaviours around others. Adding money to the mix will not make everything right. You can promise yourself up front that you won't be one of those negative people. You will be more comfortable about making money if you do that. It will be another one of your values aligned that will provide you with the freedom to take action when the time is right for you.

When some people become wealthy, there can be doubts about the motivations others have for being around them. There are plenty of examples of paranoia among the wealthy. It is hardly surprising. There are con men (and women) out there who really are out there to run off with other people's money. There are people who (sadly) are only out for what they can get. Those people aren't nice, they aren't ethical, and they aren't honest. You can decide now to be a *nice* person with money, not just a person with money. Nice does not mean naive though. You have to keep your wits about you without becoming paranoid. There is no point in having money if you live in fear of its effect on you.

It is hardly surprising that some successful pop stars, movie stars and millionaire business people end up staying closest friends with childhood friends and family. Those people can be trusted to like them for *who* they are, not for what they have.

The most important thing to take from all this is to take full personal responsibility for how you treat others. By taking full personal financial responsibility for yourself, you have options. You can make choices about how you influence others, and about who can influence you. When you put wealth and a kind heart together, you really can have the happiness that you are looking for.

Kindness is king. Never forget it.

Snap the Restraints for Good

"The purpose of life is to live it, to taste experience to the utmost, to reach out eagerly and without fear for newer and richer experience."
—Eleanor Roosevelt

Before you move onwards to designing your new financial life, this is a good time to have a quick review of how far you have come already. You already know more about how you can manage your thoughts, and you probably have a different perspective on a lot of issues that you didn't understand before. You also have a new way of looking at so many of the obstacles that, up until now, have probably been holding you back. You have a new toolbox of strategies that you can apply to your life so that you can take better control over your own happiness and your own effectiveness, and you have probably even started to make sense of why some things have been difficult for you in the past. I hope that you have a new appreciation of why it is such a fantastic time for you to develop and thrive as a person.

You also now realise the real need to respect your money. You have found out that it **is** really possible for you to break free from limiting beliefs and attitudes that you may have unwittingly brought into your adult life from your upbringing. You have greater insight into the powerhouse of your values, and now have a greater understanding how they drive so many of the things that you think and do. You know that your beliefs can be anything you want them to be, and that you need to work on developing an attitude that serves you, and that benefits those around you at the same time. You have found out that we all get in our own way sometimes, and with practice you can use new skills to stop any tendencies to sabotage your own success. You have realised that you don't have to be perfect at everything all the time. Instead, you just need to strive to be best that you can be. It is good enough! You have discovered that being kind to yourself and finding your true purpose will give you the motivation and the energy that you need to realise your dreams.

You have come to terms with the certain knowledge that your journey is going to be a struggle sometimes, but that those struggles will help you to grow more resilient over time, and you have more tools than ever before to deal with problems when things don't go your way. That's not all. You have the opportunity to decide the sort of person you want to be when you have a lot of money and know that you can use your money as a force for good through your behaviour.

So, after all that, you are ready to move on. It's time to use all of those things to break free from the shackles of debt. Here is a simple way to remember the core things that you are going to need to do from now on, a way to find your FREEDOM:

Face up to it!

Responsibility; take personal responsibility for your own finances

Erode your debts until you are debt free

Enjoy yourself as you go along

Decide to be happy – don't wait until you have "enough" money

Open yourself to new possibilities

Make some serious money!

Debts and Spending

Tethered by Temptation

"The problem is this: Often the heart and mind disagree. Fervently."
—Chip and Dan Heath, Switch: How to Change Things When Change is Hard

Why do so many people find it so easy to spend money yet so hard to save it?

Before we go into the mechanics of getting your finances on track, it is worth spending a little time looking at the hidden drivers that can cause people to get into trouble in the first place. You may recognise some of them. If you do, then understanding will give you some extra tools to use to influence your own financial behaviour like never before. You may also be able to help others, too.

If you skipped over the quote at the beginning of this chapter, take a look again now. These words were borrowed from Chip and Dan Heath's great book *Switch*, and the quote summarises the simple reason why it can be so difficult to control our buying urges and to all too easily give in to temptation.

The reality is this. We are all pulled by two opposing forces much of the time. When you are trying to manage your money, those opposing forces

are often at work inside you.. One part of you knows that you need to practice restraint, while another part of you is pulling you towards whatever
shiny thing or experience it is that you want. They are exactly the same
forces at work as when you are fighting internally about eating a piece of
great looking cake; part of you wants the cake, another part of your wants
to be slim and glamorous. This is the battle between your emotions and
your logic. These two opposing forces are inside you struggling for suprem-
acy, and they are tugging you in opposite directions a good deal of the time.

Your emotions are the strongest forces that you have, but if you don't
control them with some logic (or some other useful restraints), they can get
you into a whole heap of trouble.

Scientific testing on children has proven that the better kids are at controlling or directing their emotions, the more successful they become as
adults. Success has more to do with your ability to get the force that serves
you best to dominate your actions, than it does with having a high IQ or
being incredibly talented.

Your money management abilities are likely to be stricken with the same
emotion versus logic battle. With some advance planning and knowledge
of what's going on inside you (and outside too) you can regain control of
your money.

It is pretty obvious that sometimes you just have to take control of your
emotional spending urges; you have to take responsibility for not giving
into them. Though here's the thing: the Heath brothers discovered that we
all have a limited amount of control available to us. We literally run out
of steam in the battle over our own emotional restraint. They found out
that we can only go so far in controlling ourselves and that the answer, in
part, is to take yourself out of harm's way before the (spending) event. For
example, if you are broke, don't go shopping with your friends at the weekend, go round to their house for coffee instead. In the real world, you can't
always engineer a situation to the point where you can stay out of danger
altogether, but you can learn ways to direct your emotions, rather than
suppress them altogether.

In *Switch*, Chip and Dan use a metaphor for these two opposing forces:
the rider and the elephant. The rider is your logical mind, and the elephant
represents your emotions. They point out that although the rider likes to
think she is in charge, the elephant is the one with the power. The rider is

always smarter ahead of time, but when the elephant spots something she really wants, the rider doesn't have the power to fight it.

The Heath brothers recommend you have a strategy ready ahead of time that you can use when you know you are going to be faced with a hard decision. So if you know you can't avoid going shopping with a friend, have your rider (logical mind) plan an anti-spending strategy before you go out, when temptation isn't right in front of your eyes trying to attract your inner elephant. That is the best time to get the beast under control.

So you could try something like this next time you are tempted to spend money you don't have, for something you don't really need, to impress people you don't like. Instead of just trying to bring logic into the fray (which you now know won't always help), engage your emotions instead. When the object of your desire is right in front of you, take a moment to stop and imagine the feeling in the pit of your stomach that you will have when your credit card statement drops onto the doormat. Create that feeling of dread that you know you will experience when you have to open the envelope. The one that's especially strong when you know that earlier in the month, you added to your debts when you shouldn't have done. Live the feeling of the debt in advance. You know the feeling is going to happen if you give in to temptation. It's not in question that the feeling is going to be real sooner or later if you keep spending—it's just the case that you need to tap into the feeling ahead of time. Learn to make use of it instead of denying it when it's convenient. In other words, engage as many negative emotions as you can about the delayed effect of your behaviour at the time of temptation. Really picture how you would feel to have your debit card declined at the till of the supermarket tomorrow; sense the embarrassment of having the other shoppers staring at you as they wait in line to pay.

When you have turned up the feeling of the potential effect of spending the money that you don't need to spend, look at the object of your desire again and see if it still has the same shine. You might find that it is a whole lot easier to walk away after that! Now you know that the emotion versus logic battle can be loaded in your favour. You can increase your odds of winning and moving towards wealthy behaviour. Start to use that knowledge from now on to change how you deal with temptation.

If you haven't been successful to this point in looking after your finances as well as you would have liked, you can take heart from the fact that all this time your elephant has been dragging you down the wrong path. You know that without some tools to help you get the job done, it was not going to happen for you. You can start to feel better about yourself. You haven't been weak if you have financial problems, you have just been human!

Now you have a greater understanding of what pulls you off course and how you can resist the temptation of getting dragged down a dangerous path in the future, and you can increase the likelihood of making a big change. And you can start right now because you have so much more at your disposal.

There is one more thing to look at before we look at the practicalities of your future money management. You need to start thinking differently about debt. You have been educated that debt is a normal part of life, you and the rest of the population of the western world. Just so you know—debt is not a normal part of life. Not for you anyway, not anymore.

Keep your goal at the front of your mind as you read on. That goal is to get you out of debt so that you can begin your journey towards wealth and security. To do that, you need to know some of the things that the world is throwing at you every day. So let's move on to that right now.

The Manacles of Modern Debt Culture

"Don't borrow money unless you really, really have to. And even then don't."
—Richard Templar, The Rules of Wealth[3]

So what is going on, what else beyond our own emotions pushes so many women to spend too much and get into debt?

We are taught to borrow money, even when we know we shouldn't, in part because we are constantly bombarded by retailers and marketers telling us we can have what we want—and we can have it now! They tell us that we don't need to wait! Buy that sofa, buy it now, have it home in time for Christmas and pay for it next year. Or there is the car dealer who lets you have that shiny car on 'cheap' credit. The list goes on and on. Sooner or later, people get so laden with monthly debt repayments that they need their credit card just to go food shopping.

All you need to do is want it badly enough, and someone will make money by finding a way to let you have it. Someone gets paid handsomely for giving you instant gratification; however, that instant gratification comes at a price. A very high price.

If you are in debt, it is simply because you bought something that you couldn't afford. Someone else actually let you do that. They endorsed your behaviour by giving you access to money that you hadn't earned. Many of us still have fairly easy access to credit; our modern consumer society depends on it. It might not be quite so easy as it was in the credit-fuelled 00's, but it is still relatively easy. It is easy because people always want to make money out of other people's impatience. It is one market that will NEVER dry up. Recession or boom time, people always want what they want—and most people want it before they can afford it. That's why most people are destined to stay poor.

One of the biggest current threats is from payday lenders who have almost ridiculously lax checking procedures. Now that traditional banks have tightened up their lending policies because of government pressure, the door has blown wide open and allowed in companies who charge average interest rates of 4000% and more to lend money until the end of the month. I have even read one rate of 16 million percent. Seriously. Rates like that are no joke, but they are legal in the UK.

Just because someone else (and credit card companies count here) allows you spend more than you have, it does not remove your own personal responsibility for spending the money. They might have given you access to the money, but in most cases, you weren't forced to spend it.

You already know that the emotional aspects of spending can never be underestimated. We touched upon that in the last chapter when I explained about the rider and the elephant. Most spending decisions beyond bills are emotional ones—elephant spending. If you are feeling good, you want to celebrate it. We have been culturally trained to treat ourselves for every little triumph. If life is going well, why not celebrate with a nice dinner out, or a nice bottle of wine? If you feel bad, research shows that many women spend in an attempt to feel better. Well, they might feel better while they are trying on the dress, but they won't feel better when the bill comes in.

Picture the woman who has just been given a big promotion at work, with a salary rise to go with it. She feels great and decides she needs to go shopping to 'invest' in better clothes for work, because she will be mixing in better circles. So she buys new clothes in anticipation of all the important meetings she is going to have to go to. But she hasn't earned the money yet! Part of her salary rise gets spent before she has earned it, so she has to put the clothes on her credit card. The strange thing is that this scenario could appear to make sense. But hear this: **It doesn't make sense**. As a good friend of mine likes to say, if it's on your ass, it's not an ass-ett. What if the company she worked for went bust? Her increased salary would stop overnight. The promised promotion wouldn't exist for long; it wouldn't be there when her job was outsourced to China, but the credit card company would still be wanting to get paid for the clothes that she bought for the meetings she no longer had to go to. That credit card account wouldn't get sent to China with the job, would it? We all need to start seeing the twisted logic fed to us by the credit system for what it is.

As twisted as that might seem, it's a common spending behaviour. If that's you, can you hear how crazy that all sounds now? That's because it is crazy! So just stop it. Get a grip on crazy.

I was watching a TV programme recently that demonstrated how deeply engrained in our culture such bizarre ways of thinking have become. So bizarre that they are accepted as totally normal.

During the programme, the TV company had filmed a walk-in financial advice clinic being run by one of their financial experts. A young lady walked in, a 19-year-old student. She told the "expert" that she was thinking of getting a credit card, even though she had a job and could get by without one, and asked her advice on what she should do. The "expert" pointed out that her only income was from her student loan so she should get a bigger overdraft. Are you thinking what I'm thinking here? Anyway, she carried on. The "expert" suggested that she should get a credit card so that she could build her credit rating. Wouldn't it have been better advice to keep her spending under control and get another part time job instead of finding out from the "expert" the cheapest way of getting into debt? She was still at university for goodness sake! She was years away from finishing her course. There would be plenty of time to build her credit rating in case she decided to buy a house when she got older. It would have been a better suggestion to just warn her to stay out of debt altogether until she started work and only then to take on any debt with care, planning and for a clear reason, like getting a mortgage. I was horrified to realise just how ingrained it is in our culture that getting into debt is considered a normal part of growing up.

Everything around us is telling us that getting into debt early in life is a *way* of life and that getting a credit card is a good way of getting into a bigger debt (a mortgage), later on. This twisted logic is considered normal. It's not normal. It's another brand of crazy. The trouble with the advice about getting a credit card to build our credit rating is that research has proven that as soon as we have one, we tend to spend more. The elephant gets to take over.

When consumption becomes easy, we do more of it. Research shows, for example, people almost always leave a bigger tip when they pay a restaurant bill with a credit card than they do when they pay in cash. One study showed that people are prepared to pay twice as much for scarce tickets to a football game when they can put the cost of the tickets on their credit card, compared with what they are prepared to bid for the same tickets when they have to pay in cash.

Put simply, if more credit is available, we spend more. If we have credit in more than one place, we spend even more. Every time we put another credit card in our wallet, we make our spending possibilities bigger. We pig out on credit. The elephant can get her trunk deeper into the trough, and the animals live happily ever after. The debtor doesn't though, because the animals inside us that get us into trouble aren't so good at paying the money back.

I had a pretty shocking encounter recently that demonstrates just how bad it can get when personal spending gets out of control. I was viewing a property to buy as an investment recently. I have money that needs to work hard, and property is one of my longer-term investment strategies. I don't sit around doing nothing very often, so I don't expect my money to sit around doing nothing either.

This property was competitively priced because it had been repossessed by the bank; it was sitting empty and it had to go. It was a sweet house located in a desirable tree-lined street. It had a cute exterior, a pretty garden, and was an ideal house for a family with kids or a professional couple looking for space to spread out before they moved onto the next rung of the property ladder.

As always with a repossessed house, I felt a twinge of sadness when I walked through the front door. When I found my way into the kitchen, I saw the blue 'Do not use' tape the bailiffs had plastered across the sink. There was a glaring space where the cooker had been and the tiles were damaged where the appliances had been ripped out. It all added to the sense of pointless destruction. The estate agent explained that the bank had repossessed the house a few weeks earlier, and unless it was sold quickly, it was to be sold at auction the following month. The bank was open to offers. I told the agent how I always felt so sorry for the people who had been evicted, even though I didn't know them. She looked bemused, and then I was knocked sideways by her response.

She told me that she used to feel uncomfortable about repossessions too, in the early days of her job, but not anymore. "Our agency deals with a lot of these," she said. "I think most city agents do. We often have to value the property for the bank before the people move out, and you get a good idea of how they have been living. We did the same with this one; we saw the house before they got kicked out."

"Occasionally I see someone who is really struggling. The poor people who have lost their jobs or got sick. Those ones are pretty heartbreaking, but we don't come across too many of those," she went on. "Most of the time, that's not the way it is. We have often been trying to sell a house for an unrealistic price for a long time before they get repossessed. You know, the family using their house to try and get themselves out of trouble. They don't want to hear the realistic valuation at that point. They are in cloud cuckoo land, most of them."

"When we do valuations, we see the wardrobes full of nice clothes, there are TV's in every room. It was like that here. All the kids had an Xbox and their own iPods set up in their rooms, the kitchen was full of all the latest gadgets. It's no wonder they didn't have any money to pay their mortgage."

The estate agent got into full flow when she explained how she pays her own bills and doesn't live beyond her means. "I work full time and so does my husband, and we can't live like these people did. They choose their priorities, and I can't let it get to me. Selling houses is my job. It's not my job to feel bad if they can't control themselves. If they choose to buy all this stuff, then they must realise it will catch up with them one day. I have been dealing with one or two of these a month for years, and the story is nearly always the same."

It doesn't make pleasant reading, does it? This is clearly not an isolated incident. No wonder estate agents can be so cynical. I almost felt sorry for her! Seriously, they don't have such an easy job sometimes.

Whenever I view a repossessed house or flat, I feel a bit uncomfortable, but I can't help thinking how easily it could have been me if I hadn't learned the rules of money.

So do you feel better when you spend more on credit? While you are in the shop, when you get it out of the wrapping paper, maybe you feel better for a few minutes. The first time you wear it you might get a bit of a good feeling until you stop noticing you are wearing new clothes. But the good feeling about the purchase fades pretty quickly. Life returns to how it was before you bought it. How do you feel when the bill drops through the letterbox? Does that feeling fade with time as well? Almost certainly not. Knowing that you have pigged out on credit doesn't feel any better as time goes on. It just gets worse. You just feel sick every time you think about it.

It can be addictive. If you are addicted, you can stop. You MUST stop. Don't end up like that family who got kicked out of their house. I bet they didn't expect to get put out onto the street when they bought their big TV.

So what other reasons, apart from the availability of credit, causes us to be tempted to spend more? The answer to that is simple. It is a lack will to wait for something until you can honestly afford it. So why do we buy when we can't really afford it? Why do we have so much difficulty controlling the urge to spend?

Why is delaying gratification so hard? Let's find out.

Imprisoned by Unfettered Spending?

"The shortest period of time lies between the minute you put some money away for a rainy day, and the unexpected arrival of rain."

—Jane Bryant Quinn

I s spending your nemesis? Has it caused problems for you?

If spending has been a problem for you, you now know some of the reasons you used to do it. You know how your brain conspires against you with that eternal battle between your heart and your head.

The next step is to really face up to some of the habits that allowed you to get into trouble and face up to the uncomfortable truth about your spending. It's time for you to get out of denial.

Do you think that you are in denial about any aspects of your finances? If you answer yes to any of the following questions, you almost certainly are.

- Do you ever go shopping for clothes or shoes when you are overdrawn?
- Do you buy your kids toys for Christmas instead of paying an important bill?
- Do you ever go out for a drink or a meal when you are close to getting behind on your debt payments?

- Do you ever spend money you shouldn't so that you can keep up appearances to others?
- Do you buy things you could live without when you are struggling to pay your rent or mortgage?

It's not just the spending element of your finances that you can be in denial about either. If you are moving through life without a clear financial plan, you are in denial about needing one.

If you get your pay and then spend until you run out, you are in denial about investing for the future.

If are you earning money from employment or your own business and aren't saving for a rainy day, you are in denial about the financial thunderstorm that will one day soak you to the skin.

You really don't want to end up like the family I saw in a recent TV documentary. The general idea was to get the viewer to fume about the behaviour of the banks in the recession, but I just fumed at the denial of the participants. In this programme, I saw one of the worst cases of denial I had ever witnessed, and it showed just how quickly people can go from believing they are financially comfortable to walking over a cliff.

The family concerned had moved into a bigger house to accommodate their growing family. The husband owned a company that employed 20 electricians working on various building sites across their local city. The recession had hit, the building trade had dropped like a stone and his biggest client had stopped paying its bills. They had been used to taking nice family holidays, living in a big house in a very expensive area and driving nice cars. In other words, they had a pretty good lifestyle until crisis after crisis had hit their finances. They had secured a 100% mortgage when times we're good and banks were lending freely. When things got really tough, one of the measures that they had taken was that they sold one of their cars. The programme was being filmed as their beloved Mercedes was driven away by its new owner. What do you think they used the proceeds for? To pay some debt? To pay something to their mortgage company? Nope, none of the above.

They used the money from the car to pay for Christmas!

They had obviously been in denial for so long it had become normal. They blamed the recession, they blamed the banks, they blamed property prices. Yet when it came to the crunch, they used a bit of extra money to buy presents!

They were living in a house that they thought of as their own, but in reality they were just renting it from the bank. As they had no financial stake in the house, why would the bank believe that they had any chance of recovering the value of the property that they had lent almost half a million pounds against, and when money was tight the family were showing few (if any) signs of restraint?

Like most families they were permanently living only a small number of weeks away from potential disaster. They had no rainy day fund. It was a family tragedy. After years of living well (on other people's money), I couldn't help wondering why they had bought cars and holidays and hadn't been paying capital down to reduce their mortgage debt.

If you are in denial, admit it to yourself RIGHT NOW. If you don't, it is just a matter of time before your denial catches up with you.

You know about your elephant now, you know about the cost of denial, but before we move on to the techniques you can use to dig yourself out of a hole, we will take one final look at what dirty tricks and dark forces are trying to get access to the spending animal inside you. This is the final step in getting your personal protection water tight.

Marketing Tricks and Wealth Illusions

"If women didn't exist, all the money in the world would have no meaning."
—Aristotle Onassis

Make no mistake, if you don't have full awareness of how your emotions pull you towards certain items and brands, the manufacturers and retailers certainly do. Big companies employ psychologists, behavioural scientists, advertising agencies and professional persuaders to get their hands on your money.

They spend fortunes to understand how the human brain—your brain—processes colour, contrasts price, buys according to values, your social group and more. The advertising budgets of the multinationals are almost as big as the gross domestic product of a small country. Their experts know which types of voices and music alter your brainwaves, and slow your blink rate down so that you get to see more of their wares.

This is what you are up against every day when you are trying to make rational decisions about your purchasing and to control your finances. Businesses, from the shops on your local high street to the big car and chocolate manufacturers, spend hundreds of millions of pounds each year to attach a feel-good factor in you to their products.

There is an entire industry built around generating a desire in you to buy shiny and tasty things. Car manufacturers are particularly good at appealing to your emotions. More specifically, car branding and marketing works on the science of social proof more than any other industry. Even the price points of certain cars are designed to ensure that people with specific income levels can buy them, and that people outside those income levels shouldn't. Branding is social proof. It's how we identify and measure ourselves and how we compare ourselves to the Joneses.

Here is something that you really need to know: wealthy people buy for *different reasons*. Let me explain.

Let's look at car companies as an example. Car companies are trying to get you to buy a big ticket item that you are going to live with for a long time. Not only have you got to buy it at great expense, but you have to be pleased with it a long time after your purchase. They want to win your loyalty, and much of their advertising is geared towards your happiness AFTER purchase. They want to keep you coming back for servicing, repairing and eventually replacing your car. They need that follow through from you because they need to keep their dealer network in business, as well as their factories. So they want you to *keep on* feeling good about your buying decision, long after you have made it. Motor manufacturers understand that buyer's remorse makes people feel bad, and they don't want those bad feelings being attached to *their* cars. You need to realise that you are being sold at nearly all the time. You are being shamelessly targeted to part with your cash. It will always be the case, and there will always be something you can't have. Just get used to it.

When it comes to money and wealth, appearances are deceptive. You never know these days, when you see someone driving a fancy car if it is paid for in full, or still on credit. The car (or the shoes, or the suit, or the holiday destination, or the house), tells you very little about the person who has it. It may tell you that they have an excellent money management strategy and are genuinely wealthy, or (knowing the average householder debt figures in both the UK and US), it is more likely that it just tells you that they have more debt than you.

What the car won't tell you is that they might be buckling under the strain of tens of thousands of debt. That BMW doesn't tell you that they may only be weeks away from going under. What the car really says about them as people is meaningless. In our credit-driven society, a nice car no longer means anything concrete. In fact, it doesn't tell you anything meaningful at all. All it tells you is that the person who has the car/shoes/holiday *wishes* they could afford it. It certainly does not tell you that they **can** afford it!

Train yourself to live within your means. It is the only way to get wealthy. One of the easiest ways to do it is to use cash instead of plastic. It's impossible to overspend cash. When you run out, that's it.

When you shop, shop to buy something specific, and if you don't have cash, don't buy anything! It is easier than you think. It just takes a bit of practice.

Whipping Your Debt Busting Skills into Shape

"I spent a lot of money on booze, birds, and fast cars. The rest I just squandered."
—George Best, footballer

So if you are in debt now, how do you get out of it?

Like all things financial, you need to plan. The first thing you need to do is cut down your spending. I know that sounds obvious, but it needs to be said. Cutting down is as much about changing your habits as it is about the money itself.

Planning is something that we are all capable of. If you don't think of yourself as a good planner, I'm going to prove to you that you are a planner already. Everyone on the planet has planning skills. It's just that not everyone can be bothered to use those skills on their finances. You are going to be different, and you are going to start now! There are some things that women just *know* how to prepare for, and we don't give them a second thought. We all have great planning skills. Planning comes naturally to us. Like getting ready for a wedding, or some event that you need get dressed up for. Such events take planning. Very few women just decide half an hour before they go out what they are going to wear. It's usually more like a military operation that starts weeks before the event. It is all about planning, and we all plan for things that we care about.

There are dozens of things that every woman does automatically that need thought and planning skills. I've pointed out just one. You probably have your own list of things you are great at planning: holidays, shopping, projects at work, cooking. Only you know your personal strengths.

So if you didn't think of yourself as a planner before now, think again. You are a great planner! Now you just need to take the skills that you already have and apply them to your finances. I read somewhere that most people spend more time planning their summer holiday than they do planning how to pay for it. Crazy comes up again. Ditch crazy; make a plan instead. It's the only way to get straight.

Our mothers, friends and our peer group help us learn so many planning skills when we are young. Every day we are given a fistful of money. Even if you are in the worst possible situation on benefits at the moment, you are still handling money all the time.

Most of us had no real education before we went out into the world with money. You wouldn't let your kids out to drive a car without lessons first, would you? You wouldn't just pop them in the driver's seat and say, "There you go, sweetie. Go teach yourself to drive and come in when you get hungry. Call me if you crash." It would be madness, an accident waiting to happen. Yet we as good as do that with money every day.

It's not necessarily your fault. If you are one of the lucky ones, your parents might have given you a few basic lessons in budgeting, and they might even have helped to teach you how to save. Unlike driving a car, to handle money you didn't need a licence. Out you went, sent out on the road to find your own way about. And your purse didn't come complete with a handbook about when and how to use it.

Now it really is time for you to get up to speed with some basic rules of the road to manage your finances. I doubt that you had the full money user manual given to you before you were first sent out into the world with some, so don't get too cross with yourself if you have got into a mess. If no one told you what to do, how could you have known?

You can get out of it if you follow a few simple rules. So let's start with understanding the true cost of debt, how much it costs, how it works and how to get out of it.

Understanding the True Cost of Debt

"Compound interest is the eighth wonder of the world. He who understands it, earns it ... he who doesn't ... pays it."
—Albert Einstein

D o you really know how much debt costs? Do you understand the principles of compound interest?

These are two big questions because, in my experience, very few people understand either the principles of how it works or the general rules of debt. Even when you get to know the rules, the financial companies like to keep changing them to keep you on your toes. Even tiny details that change about things like how much of your payments go towards interest and how much towards reducing the debt itself, tend to keep things weighted in the lender's favour. For the sake of your wealth, you must remember that your debt is there for their profit and not your convenience.

It is not often considered that one person's debt is another person's asset. Let me expand that for you. To illustrate this, imagine for a moment that you have taken out a loan for £1000. Your loan is with the The Loan Illustration Company PLC. You have a fixed rate of interest set at 10% annual percentage rate (the APR), and the loan is for one year. You therefore have been told when you took out the loan that your total obligation is worth £1000, plus one years' interest at 10%, which amounts to £100. Still with me? Good. So your obligation is for a total of £1100 because your original loan value has now been inflated by the interest charge. That extra £100 interest is worth money to someone. It has value because you may be paying 10% interest on the loan, but the provider of the money is paying considerably less interest than you are.

So now, The Loan Illustration Company PLC "owns" your debt and "owns" the income stream of £100 that is the value of your interest payment. You are now an asset on their books. You have value, because your debt has value. They can sell your debt whenever they please. That fact is usually hidden in the small print of your loan agreement. Sadly, you can't do the same and sell what you owe to someone else! The Loan Illustration Company PLC has now added value to *their* business. Now you can see why companies want your debt. Now you understand why they sometimes lend to people who can't really afford to pay it back. That's why governments regulate these industries, but not all lending is created equal in the eyes of the law. That's why you need to be so careful when you take on debt. We talk about less scrupulous lenders later on, but for now realise that not enough people appreciate that their debt is someone else's asset.

So now that you know that your debt is valuable to someone else. After all, why would someone who didn't know you lend you money if they weren't going to get something out of it? It's now time for you to look at the true cost of different types of debt.

One way that your debts can become an asset that gives a bank an "interest" in you is bank overdrafts, so we will explore these first. This form of debt can really ramp up the effect of compound interest. Compound interest is basically the interest on your interest; it can make you or break you. Remember the quote from the beginning of this chapter by Albert Einstein? Even Albert marvelled at the miraculous and disastrous effects of compound interest. Although you don't have to be Einstein to understand it, you do need to understand the impact it can have on you.

Bank overdrafts are probably the form of lending that takes greatest benefit from compound interest—if you are the bank of course. If you are the borrower, it's a different kettle of fish. The reasons for this are twofold. Firstly, the rates of interest on overdrafts are high, and secondly, because of the speed and frequency at which both any charges and interest payments are added to the balance of your debt.

There are two types of overdrafts, authorised and unauthorised. Authorised overdrafts are when you have pre-agreed with the bank that you are going to go into the red, and they grant a pre-agreed limit of how much money they will let you have until they start to bounce your payments. These rates can easily be up to 40 times the base interest rate. The base interest rate is the rate that is set by the central bank wherever you live. In the UK, that would be the Bank of England, and in the United States, it is the Federal Reserve. That is truly scary. Most people surveyed don't even know the rate their bank charges them when they go overdrawn. Unauthorised overdrafts are even worse. This is when there is no pre-agreed borrowing with the bank, but you go overdrawn anyway. The rates are penal. Much unauthorised borrowing happens when people don't keep track of direct debits or bank charges leaving their account, putting them accidentally in the red. Charges can be excruciating for every failed transaction. Failed transactions cost a fortune, and remember, the bank doesn't pay a failed transaction, but you do get charged for the rejected payment anyway. A single failed payment of less than £10 can easily attract a rejection charge of £25 or more. Interest is charged on these charges too. This multiplies the speed at which the debt grows, and it's a downward spiral that is hard to escape from if you don't understand the costs.

The reason overdrafts are so good at accumulating compound interest for the banks is this. Interest is calculated daily, and from the moment the interest is added to the debt, more interest starts being charged on it—interest on the interest. Then there is the interest on the charges. Then there is interest on the interest on the charges. Things can escalate out of control for the borrower with frightening speed.

These days, many banks charge a daily fee for overdrafts. It used to be monthly. It is yet another way to make more money, more often, from your debts. Keith Tondeur, chief executive of the money education charity Credit Action, commented on the results of a UK money survey on TalkTalk's money news website:

This survey throws up some really frightening figures and trends. Millions of us are permanently living beyond our means and the lack of even basic money education means most of us haven't the faintest idea how much this is costing us. Overdrafts have gone from being a facility to use in an emergency to something we depend on. Whilst some of the blame for this can be laid at the lenders' door it also says something about the "short-termism" and instant gratification culture that engulfs our society. The survey results for young adults are particularly alarming.

So now for the next most common form of debt. It is time to move on to looking at the cost of credit card borrowing. For illustration purposes, let's go imaginary shopping for a moment. Let's say you bought a dress that cost you £100, a pair of shoes and a bag that cost another £100. That's a total spend of £200. If you buy all the items for cash, the cost is £200 and will always be £200. When you give them to the charity shop when they have gone out of fashion, you are giving away £200 worth of goods. Hopefully you will have had your money's worth by then. But what happens to the overall cost to you when you put that same dress, shoes and bag on a credit card and "spread" the cost?

I need to make a couple of assumptions to illustrate this with a level of realism. First of all, I have assumed you have an average credit rating and that your interest rate is a conservative 18%. That is considerably below many credit card rates at the time of writing but not the absolute cheapest rate.

If you pay the minimum payment of £5 per month, it would take you 4 years and 11 months to clear the debt. That shopping would cost you a total of £294.00.[4] You would be paying almost half the cost of the goods again in interest. Suddenly, "saving money" by going shopping in the sales and putting the "bargain" on your credit card doesn't seem so appealing does it?

By the time you had paid off the debt, the dress will probably have either fallen out of fashion or fallen apart. Just like your finances.

In the UK, the average consumer borrowing (including credit cards, motor and retail finance deals, overdrafts and unsecured loans) per UK adult was £3,218 in February 2013. Let's be nice and round that down to £3000. Repaying that amount by only forking out the minimum payment would take you more than 27 YEARS.

Read that again. 27 years, and that's assuming that interest rates never go up. That's one assumption that I can guarantee is a bad one. Interest rates always go up eventually. They are currently at record low levels but will not stay like that for the next 27 years.

You would also pay £3961[5]—in interest alone. That's significantly more than **doubling** the original debt. The reason that credit cards can take so long to pay off is this. When you pay minimum payments, you are *almost* taking out an interest only loan. The part of the payment that is allocated by the credit card company to paying back the original purchase itself is only a tiny proportion of the payment. Most if the payment is interest.

The lesson to take from all this is simple. You must avoid, AT ALL COSTS, paying the minimum payments on credit card debt. Of course, you should get rid of it all together, and we will get to that. In the meantime, pay a fixed sum while you are paying your cards down.

If you don't fix your payment to an amount, and you let the credit card company decide the minimum payment, what happens is this. Each time you repay some debt, the minimum payment goes down. In effect this gives the credit card company longer to hang onto the debt so that they can earn more money from you.

I'll give you an illustration of what happens. Let's take that same £3,000 debt at 17.9% interest, with minimum repayments of 1% of the balance plus interest. In the first month, your minimum repayment would be just over £71. If instead of just paying the minimum, you repaid the same £71 every month, it would (only!) take you five years to pay off and the interest cost would be £1,500; a saving of over £2,400. Not only that, you take almost 20 YEARS off the time it takes to pay back the debt. Read that again, 20 YEARS less to pay it off. Now can you see why you must **never pay minimum** payments. It is a hell hole so deep that you can't imagine how long it will take you to get out.

The more you pay each month, the less you pay in total and the shorter the payment period will be. If you want to get wealthy, your aim needs to be to get debt free, and stay debt free.

So now, let's get down to business. I will start by explaining what you need to do *before* you can start building wealth.

The Importance of a Solid Foundation

"Annual income twenty pounds, annual expenditure nineteen [pounds] nineteen [shillings] and six [pence], result happiness. Annual income twenty pounds, annual expenditure twenty pounds and six [pence], result misery."
—Charles Dickens, David Copperfield

D o you have a stable foundation to start building your wealth, or are you still in debt at the moment?

Whatever your answer, you need to understand that you need to be financially stable before you can start to build wealth. But even if you are in debt, it is possible to be *stable*—as long as you have an income. Before I jump down into the detail, let me share three key points with you:

Reaching a point of financial stability can be THE most challenging step on your journey.

You have to get there *before* you can get any level of true wealth.

It is THE MOST liberating step of all!

Before you can get wealthy, or even comfortable, you absolutely have to get stable. It is your bedrock. That is your foundation, and being stable will allow you focus on the outcomes that you want for your future. When you get stable, a whole world of new possibilities opens up to you. The flip side you probably already know; financial instability is not only stressful, it is distracting, terrible for your mental health, can attack your physical health and do lasting damage your closest relationships.

Beyond financial instability, overwhelming levels of debt are even worse. Debt is a cancer on your well-being, and it needs invasive, radical therapy.

My definition of financial stability is simple. You are stable when:

- You consistently bring in more money than you spend
- You have enough set aside, specifically allocated to unexpected costly events (car problems, unexpected bills, etc.)

When your finances pass that test, you are stable. That's what your foundation looks like, and it's the first thing you need to have in place before you can really power forward. Having basic financial stability puts you in a position where you can weather the day-to-day storms of life that hit us all. You might get a little distracted by a gale, but you know you won't be blown too far off course by it. Storms do hit, they hit everyone. It's usually the case that they have a habit of hitting at the worst possible moment. That's just a fact of life, so you need to protect yourself ahead of time. My husband's favourite phrase is "being robust in the face of uncertainty".

If you aren't stable yet, you probably realise that you need to do more than just change your thinking. You need to take some practical steps to put your own bedrock in place. So here is where you start to get practical.

You need to get your head around the fact that you will have to work to a budget. It's not very rock and roll, I know. But hey, rock and roll isn't very rock and roll sometimes. Every business has its bit of drudgery, and you need to start thinking of yourself as a walking business. Once you accept that, and embrace it, then it's fun. Lots of fun.

So now that you know a useful definition of a stable foundation, let's move on to how you build yours.

How to Build a Solid Foundation

"A successful man is one who can lay a firm foundation with the bricks others have thrown at him."
 —David Brinkley

S o exactly how do you go about laying a firm foundation?
 The answer is elegant in its simplicity. You put yourself in a
 position where you earn more than you spend. That's it. But in the
western world, we have been brought up to be almost trained to be in debt.
Credit cards, student loans, mortgages and hire purchase. Even the interest
free credit peddled by stores is still debt; and you already know the true
cost of debt.

Even then, earning more than you spend can be hard to do, especially if
you have got out of the habit of living within your means. If you want to be
wealthy, you have to change your habits. You have to learn to live within
your means.

So let's look at your options to create your own firm foundation, your
bedrock of financial stability. First of all, you look beyond the problem.
Instead of just looking at stability, let's look to where that inevitably leads.
It leads to wealth. That's because if you get into the right habits, for the

right reasons, you will continue to accumulate money. So to become stable, to build your foundation, you can either:

- Make more money—without spending any more than you do currently
- Make the same amount as you do now but SPEND LESS, or
- Make more money **AND** spend less AT THE SAME TIME

You need to move to route three as quickly as you can. To make the gap between how much you bring in and how much you spend as big as possible, and do it as quickly as possible. Once you are there, and stay there, you will have your foundation, and if you keep doing it, over time you will become more and more wealthy.

It's not rocket science, is it? There is no other way. Yet if it is that simple, why doesn't everyone do it?

There are lots of reasons. Our culture of wanting things immediately is one reason, but the biggest one of all is this. Whichever route you take to wealth requires each person to take full personal responsibility. That takes enormous courage for one thing. On top of that it takes focus, tenacity and work. Probably a lot of work, and very hard work! The difference is that unlike people who do a little work on the minimum of effort for a long time, you can design it so that you do maximum work on maximum effort for a shorter time. All that effort is more than many people want to give. They want an easy life. It's such a shame, because what those people don't realise is that the rewards go way beyond the money itself. The money is just a by-product. It just happens.

If you do take on the challenge, eventually you do get an easier life. A more fun life. A more fulfilling life. Hard work is easy, when you love what you are doing. Life does become easier when your money is working harder than you. But for those who don't take personal responsibility, they always have to work for their money. They don't get it. They are living life the wrong way round!

You can't buy personal responsibility—and yet it's worth a fortune. That's the irony of it. People who decide to take it earn more individually than the combined income of the thousands who don't! They are the thousands who want an easy life without the work, the ones who want to live now and pay later, they are the ones who complain that life is 'unfair', the government is unfair, taxes are unfair and that everything is stacked against them.

If I had to sum up the single greatest secret to getting out of debt and going on to create wealth, taking personal responsibility for your own outcomes is it.

You need to take personal responsibility for *how* you think, *what* you think AND what you *do*. So let's start with some systems for getting your spending under control. You have the right mindset now; all you need are the tools. The aim is that one day you will be able to do as you wish with your money without worrying about it, right? To do that, you must control your spending now. Here are some tools for you, so you can start to do just that.

Start with Some Savings

"Remember, if you ever need a helping hand, it's at the end of your arm, as you get older, remember you have another hand: The first is to help yourself, the second is to help others."
—Audrey Hepburn

Even if you are in debt, you are going to need to start building some savings. Bizarre as it may seem, you are going to do that **before** you do anything else. Although that might sound odd, there is good reason for it. Let me explain why this "save first, debt down later" approach works.

It works because disaster always strikes when you are broke. I don't know why it works like that, it just does. Not only does disaster strike, but the more broke you are, the harder it strikes, the deeper the wound and the longer it goes on for. That's how it is when you don't have any back up plans.

I remember when I was trying to clamber back from being deeply in debt. It always felt as if I was pushing a rock up a hill, and as soon as I seemed to get near the top of the hill, *wallop* some bill would land on the doormat to send me scuttling back to the bottom of the hill again. That was until I followed the system of save first, debt down later.

I recently read Dave Ramsey's great book *The Total Money Make Over*, and he also advocates this very method of saving before doing anything else. He refers to it as a rainy day fund, and there is no better simple term, we all understand it without further explanation. Dave's lessons have helped millions get out of debt, and here's the interesting thing. It is almost the same method that I worked out for myself, several years before the book was published. I can tell you from experience; you need a rainy day fund. Having one does work. It will smooth your journey.

It works because it will do two things for you. First of all, it will stop you from backsliding further into debt if a big bill comes in, and second, it will make you feel better the moment you know it's there. It is your first bit of security. Do not be tempted to break into it for anything except genuine emergencies. It's not there to dip into it for a new dress or to buy Christmas presents for the kids. Neither of those things are emergencies.

I recommend that you start with a rainy day fund of £900 and do it as quickly as possible. Save every penny until you have it. Sell stuff on eBay, take a part time job, anything. Just get the rainy day fund in place. There is a reason for it being £900 too. If you start with less than that, then one big repair bill will wipe it out and destroy your resolve; if you have to spend it on one big bill, you are likely to give up on your road to wealth before you even get started.

To try to save £1000 is too intimidating if you are in debt at the moment. It's just too big a mountain to climb, too many zeros. So start with £900. Even if you are in debt, even if you are struggling financially, having this cushion will bring you an enormous sense of relief. To save it, you may have to do something that you have never done before—write down a budget. So, it's time for budgeting. We were always going to have to deal with it sometime; so here goes.

The World's Easiest Budgeting System

"It's clearly a budget. It's got lots of numbers in it."
—George W. Bush

Do you work with, and stick to, a budget as a matter of routine?
If you do, that's great, but if you don't, you need to if you want to control your finances. There is no way to avoid handling money while you are getting ready to launch your new life of financial freedom.

If you are in debt at this point in time, you still need to live from day to day. So instead of going down the usual money management route, of fully dealing with repayment of your debts first, I'm going to start with dealing with how money flows in and out of your possession. Because if you don't deal with that first, it will be impossible to ever pay your debts off.

You need a budget. If you don't have one, the simple fact of the matter is this: your money is in control of you when it should be the other way round. Remind yourself that if you want to have something different, you need to do something different. Having a budget is simply about getting the upper hand over your money. It is all about regaining control.

You need to *be* in control to *feel* in control. If you don't have a budget, then you are always capable of being taken by surprise by your money. Don't let it rule you like that—it's your money, start telling it what to do!

To manage your cash you will need to have some basic budgeting skills, because you don't need to overspend by much to be unhappy and broke.

Before I delve into the details of the system, you need to get your head around the simplest trick of all; you are going to start to use cash. We all have so many financial products and ways of paying for things these days, and fewer and fewer of us are using cash. We use debit cards, credit cards, mobile phones, PayPal and internet banking. They all have their place, but there is a big risk with these diverse payment methods. It can be all too easy to lose track of your expenditure, and the more payment options you have, the easier it gets to lose track.

You will be surprised that when you start to use cash as your first line of defence, how it will help you think twice before spending money, even small amounts. Laziness or lack of time becomes an asset. If you haven't got time to go and get cash out, you can't buy anything. Using cash as your default payment method will soon start to make you think harder than ever about buying things that you don't **really** need. There's something very real about parting with paper money. Parting with real cash is somehow much more of an emotive thing to do than the alternatives. Putting your debit card or credit card into a machine doesn't really feel like spending for many people.

So start to use cash. It will help you get back on track; it will help you to stay on track. We are going to look at how you manage that cash in a moment, but before we get to that, let's dig a bit deeper so if you have any lingering doubts you can push them out of the way.

Here is your first skill test question. How good are you with numbers? If you are already recoiling in horror at the thought of working with numbers, using cash and working to a budget, allow me to give you some encouragement. You really don't need to be good with numbers, I'm not. That might surprise you. You might even be asking yourself how someone who is rubbish with numbers has the skills to be good with money and to give you guidance about yours.

I can confidently say, from a position of authority, that it doesn't need to have any negative effect on your money management. You need some basic tools and a system. That's it. You do not need to be a professor of mathematics. In fact, it is the maths whizz kids that have caused some of the biggest banking and trading losses of all time.[6] My point here is that being good with numbers is no guarantee of being good with money, and not being good with numbers is no predictor of wealth either. I'm terrible with figures but it hasn't hurt my wealth one bit. Yet looking back, my perception of my lack of skill had a serious effect on me. It's not that I can't add up, I have a calculator for that. The fact was that I had a bit of a complex. It started at school, and the maths classes which were designed to improve numeracy skills (supposedly) turned my mild aversion into a full blown crisis of confidence. It gave me an insecurity about working with numbers for years, and I allowed that to turn into a self-fulfilling prophecy when it came to my finances.

Eventually I created a system that was easy enough for my number phobic brain to manage, and when I practiced it regularly, my confidence grew over time. So you now know—you don't need to be good with numbers to be good at budgeting. So having got that out of the way, it's time to understand the details. There aren't many because this is a simple system.

Here's what you need: paper, pen, a few brown envelopes and some cash. That's it. When I did this, and refined it a little, I really started to be able to manage my money, instead of my money managing me. These days, I do have various other mechanisms to store and arrange my money, but I still use the same basic concept and keep track of my money in roughly the same way. I still always picture my money as piles of notes. So why does it works so universally well? I have asked various people over the years, and they tell me the same thing. It is the sheer simplicity of it.

Rather than give you a boring narrative of how it works and what to do, I will tell you how it came about. When you see it in action, you will be able to apply the same principles yourself. Years ago I used to have a fruit and vegetable shop. Money was tight, and I ran the business from hand to mouth on a daily basis, so I had to manage my cash if I wanted to open the shop the following day.

On a Monday I started with some money. For sake of illustration, let's say I started with £200. I went off to the wholesale market at 4 am and spent £200 on stock. I got back to the shop, put the stock on the shelves and sold most of it that day. What was left over, would get sold later in the week. On Monday night, I took the £200 back out of the till. Put it in a brown envelope and took it to the market the following morning and did the same thing again and kept doing it through until Friday morning. The last market day.

Friday and Saturday were the busiest shopping days, and the tills rang as the commuters came in and stocked up their fridges for the weekend and the week ahead. By midday on Friday, I usually had the original £200 back. The money I had started the week with. That went into an envelope marked "Monday - £200 - stock money". I knew what my overheads were. I had business property taxes, rent on the shop, wages, utilities and petrol for the van that moved the goods from market to shop. Each major expense had its own envelope. After midday on Friday, as the money came in, I filled each envelope in turn with cash to cover the cost. It was easy; when one envelope was full, I filled the next and so on. Generally, by Saturday morning I had filled them all. I knew for sure that anything that didn't have to go into an expenses envelope was profit. I didn't need an accountant to tell me how much money I made!

In those days, small traders didn't have computers. Even home PC's were years away, so a calculator, a pen and those little envelopes were the only tools available. It kept life simple. I knew how much money I needed because I wrote the amounts of the bills on the front of each envelope before Friday arrived. I knew how much I needed to take to stay solvent. I also knew, almost to the minute, what time on a Saturday I went into profit. If all the envelopes were filled by 9.30, I was going to have a great week. If I was struggling to get the expenses envelopes filled by lunchtime, I was in trouble. Steps could be taken to get things moving. I could reduce prices, send staff home early, change the window display, or put better looking produce on the street near the shop. Because I knew exactly what my position was, I could stay lean and mean.

It is very hard to do that with electronic money because most of the time you don't know what's going on. You can't adapt quickly enough. If you are running out of money, you often don't find out until you get a message from the bank telling you it has bounced a payment or that you have gone overdrawn.

For it to work for you, just list your outgoings. Give each one an envelope and make sure you find a way to fill each one before the bill goes out. It helps if you use cash because it is easier to count, and easier to keep the money for different things in different places. You can keep track of it almost without effort.

If your envelopes are full, you are OK; if they are empty, you know you are heading for trouble. You can move it all to a computer later if you wish. Trust the fact that this system can be turned electronic later on. Your envelopes can become virtual, a combination of spreadsheets and internet banking. However, I strongly recommend that you start by counting out real cash, the same way I did all those years ago. It will re-connect you to your money.

To create your budget, face up to the reality of your costs. Write a list of your most important regular weekly and monthly bills; include accommodation (rent or mortgage), property taxes, telephone/mobile costs, TV and internet costs, transport and fuel, utilities, food and groceries, credit card payments and any other regular loan or car payments. List amounts, the dates they are due and what each payment is for. Write envelopes for each category.

Next, get a clearer view of your irregular essential expenditure. Write down all the things you know you have to pay for that are due less frequently. These expenses are the ones that can most easily catch you out. They have a habit of appearing when you least expect them, and almost always when you can least afford them. Do your very best to capture everything you can think of. Include things like car tax, TV licence, insurance premiums and vaccinations for pets. These are expenses that are probably due once or twice a year. Once again, write envelopes for them.

OK. That's the horrible part done. So you can move to step three. Now you have a good picture of what you really spend.

Start filling the envelopes one by one. If you get paid into your bank account, you can still use them—even if they are physically empty. Even if they just represent how you organise what is in your bank account. They will help your organise your brain. You can get some cash out of the bank to fill them if it makes you feel better. If you haven't got enough to fill them, you can't buy new things until you have. The money that comes into your possession isn't yours until the envelopes are filled. The money in those essential envelopes is only there for you to look after until you have to hand it over.

When your envelopes are full, you can have a "spending money" envelope, and you can put money in it for yourself. That is a nice envelope to have. That money IS yours, and you can do what you like with it.

This stuff is not complicated. You just need to do it!

So, are you in the red or in the black? Are you living within your means? If you are, that's great. If you're not, then you need to find a way to reduce your expenses or earn some more money fast. In reality, you probably need to do both.

Pay for as much as you can in cash. Make as many of those envelopes as possible a temporary home for real money. Petrol, shopping, whatever. As many things as you can, that you normally pay with plastic or other means, move them to becoming cash purchases.

If you are really struggling financially, and only have tiny amounts to work with, this system works really well. Like I did with the fruit shop, you are aiming to get the envelopes filled up earlier and earlier in the week (or month), so that you have some money left over at the end of the month— instead of month left over at the end of the money!

If you have an irregular income or are self-employed, this works brilliantly. In fact, it is essential because it is impossible to overspend cash. When it's gone, it's gone for good.

So what do you do if you haven't got enough money to fill your essential envelopes all at once? Simply put the most important envelope at the top of the pile, and stuff that one first. When it's full, move onto the next envelope and continue down the pile.

Working this way helps you to prioritise your bills, and you have a clear view of your real situation on a daily basis. It is much easier than having everything in one pot (or bank account), where you have standing orders and electronic payments going out all over the place confusing the life out of you. For big bills that are always due on a certain date, it helps if you put the date on the envelope too. That's another good way of giving you a clear picture when you shuffle through your envelopes to see where you are.

These days I don't work with cash so much. Partly because I'm not in a cash business anymore, but mainly because I am disciplined and organised enough not to need to. But I have done my time!

When you are ready, you can open up bank accounts. Organise them to be as close to your cash system as possible. Make sure that they are internet enabled, so that you can move money between your accounts easily. Personally, I run seven different accounts, so I have an overview at my fingertips. I never have to remember what goes out when because each account is just a virtual brown envelope to me. I know how much money I need to stuff into each one.

If you aren't so practiced or if you haven't got a budget going yet, I strongly suggest that you don't go electronic with your money too early. Learn to manage real cash first. Stay physically and emotionally connected to your money.

Remember your rainy day fund envelope should have £900 in it. You know the importance of that.

If you have to "borrow" from one envelope to feed another because of, say, the timing of a bill, do so by all means. Just write what you have "borrowed" from yourself so you can pay it back. It's another way to keep on track that is almost impossible when you work with one pot of money in one bank account.

That's the great thing about the envelope system. These simple steps don't take more than a couple of hours to get set up, then only a few minutes a day to maintain. You can keep the system on track over a cup of tea every day.

Just give it a go. You will be up and running in minutes. It really is the world's easiest budgeting system; and having tried a fair few supposedly cleverer ones over the years, I keep coming back to it because it is so easy that it almost runs itself after a while. It becomes a habit, and all wealthy people have good money habits. If you have kids, I strongly suggest you teach them to do it with their pocket money!

Just a quick word about tax. If you are self-employed, you do need to allocate money for tax. I strongly advise that you do this *as the money comes in*. When your tax demand is due, it pays to avoid a cash shortfall at payment time. Tax is not an unexpected bill! I had a brown envelope for tax back then. These days, I still have a separate bank account. Tax is not my money, so the quicker I can't spend it by accident the better. I move it into my "tax account" as soon as I get any money in. If you are self-employed, I suggest you do the same. So how much should you put away for tax? I suggest you put around 30% of your gross profits away. That should cover the bulk of most peoples' tax liability. If it's not quite enough, then the extra amount won't be frightening, and you always have time between the bill arriving and you having to pay it, so it shouldn't be too difficult to find the extra money. If you over provision for tax, you get a nice end of year bonus.

As a generalisation, these simple habits need to become as much a part of your life as getting up in the morning. At least they do if you want to be better off than you are now. You absolutely must be able to control the flow of money in and out of your life, because if you don't, that money controls YOU.

After paying the bills, you do actually deserve some of your own money for yourself too, so let's look at how you do that next. Let's look at the subject spending money on yourself during the process of getting back on track.

Trick or Treat

"If you spend your whole life waiting for the
storm, you'll never enjoy the sunshine."
—Morris West

Some financial gurus advocate not spending a single penny on yourself, beyond absolutely essential expenditure, until after all of your
debts are paid off.

You can do that if you like, but I know that when I was £60,000 in debt,
I would never have sustained the effort for long enough to see things
through. I would have gone nuts if I had waited until I was truly solvent
before I had anything nice for myself. If I had done that, it would have been
years before I spent any money on myself. More importantly, there would
have been a real risk that I could have used spending that money as a signal
of a lapse in willpower during the process of getting out of debt. I didn't
want to set myself up for failure. So I took a totally different route, and it
worked for me.

From the first moment that I got to the point where I was earning more
money than I needed for essential costs and loan repayments, I started to put
money aside for myself. Once I had my rainy day fund in place, I started to

put 10% of my after tax earnings away for myself. Remember, I had already got to the point where I knew I had covered my essential costs. I didn't do this until I knew for sure that I wasn't getting further behind. That took about six months for me. Some people get there much faster, and some people take longer. Time is not relevant here, but the order you do it in IS.

I figured that it was me that did the work, so I should get paid!

After I had given myself a little something (and the emphasis is as strong for the "little" as it is for the "something"), I had the mental freedom to deal with the issues at hand. The issues at hand being keeping up with my bills and expenses from day to day so that I didn't get any further into debt, and also reducing the debts I had built up in the past. I paid myself first. I used that money to go away for the weekend sometimes. Other times, I bought something pretty for the house. But whatever I spent it on, I made sure that the point was to make me feel better, so I could keep up my energy and enthusiasm.

This is such a simple system, and such a good one, I strongly suggest that you copy it.

It has been thoroughly tested, not just by me, but by many others I have counselled over the years. Although 10% wasn't much, giving myself that little bit of financial freedom from the very first moment I could helped me to feel a whole lot better very quickly.

You will find your own unique way to feel better quickly so that you can sustain your efforts. That is very much what the rainy day fund is all about, and this is the logical step that runs right alongside it. If you don't have your rainy day fund yet, I suggest you wait to pay yourself until you have. That way you will get a double benefit. Doing things this way allowed me to have some money in my purse that was truly mine, and I did not have to feel guilty about it. Sometimes it was only enough for a couple of cups of great coffee at a coffee shop, but it is hard to describe just how good that coffee tasted!

I had my rainy day fund in place, I had the ability to pay my bills, I had allocated money to pay my debts and I deserved something for myself for my efforts.

Obviously, I did it by creating a brown envelope. I labelled it "spending money", and that's where I put my own 10%. It was the most fun envelope because I knew that for the first time in years, the money in it was actually mine.

If I had any of that money left over at the end of the week, I often transferred it into another envelope labelled "get there faster". I figured that I had three options with the surplus: I could spend it, let it build up in my "spending money" envelope, or I could use what I didn't spend to pay off my debts even faster. I did all three at different times; it depended on how I felt that week. Sometimes when I kept the surplus in my "spending money" envelope, I did something bigger with it like taking a last minute (cheap!) holiday, which built up my energy reserves again. Sometimes I put the money in my "get there faster" envelope. Sometimes I paid a few pounds off a debt. You need to keep a little bit of flexibility for yourself too. It was that freedom of choice, however small the amount, that encouraged me to keep going.

It was my "get there faster" envelope that really sowed the seeds for my financial independence. Even if it only contained £1, it was £1 off my debts more than I had budgeted for. I got excited about that last envelope. In fact, sometimes I got even more excited about that than I did about my spending money. I knew deep down that the quicker I filled up my "get there faster" envelope, the quicker I would be able to have more than 10% of my income going into my "spending money" envelope. These days, I only have to put about 10% of my after-tax income into my expenses envelopes. The other 90% is spending money. How cool is that!

Very few people can spend 90% of what they earn on themselves. I would like you to understand though, from that 90% that's mine, I now fund longer-term investments. I certainly don't blow it just because it's there. Only lottery winners do that. It's just the bigger the "spending money" envelope becomes, the less of it I need or want, and the greater proportion of it gets allocated to income-producing assets. That's how I get my money to work for me, instead of me working for my money. I buy assets with it. Of course, I don't spend all of the 90%; that would be a recipe for disaster—but every once in a while I go mad. It's usually on a horse. Some women love and collect shoes, I love and collect horses. But that is now; let's go back to when I only had a few pounds to play with.

It was my "get there faster" envelope that changed my habits once and for all. I discovered very quickly after I started planning and executing my budget that this envelope was my real route to freedom. I used the contents to pay something off a credit card bill. Sometimes it was only £2. Every tiny debt reduction started to give me a high. Even just £2 made me feel better than I had felt for years. Although that sounds like my own brand of crazy when you recall that my debt started off at over £60,000, I really did get a high from a measly £2 move in the right direction.

It wasn't the amount that mattered. It was the fact that I was **doing something about it** that mattered. I had made the decision to live differently. I was living differently. I knew that I was on the right track, and every £2 made it feel more real.

It is tempting to think when the numbers are small that they don't matter. It is quite the reverse. If you are in debt, you probably got into it one cup of coffee and one pair of shoes and one electricity bill at a time. So here's the best bit, you can get out of it the same way. So let's look at that now, let's get started on demolishing your debts once and for all.

Break the Shackles — Slash Those Debts

"Discipline is the bridge between thought and accomplishment… the glue that binds inspiration to achievement."
—Jim Rohn

S o now you get to the good part. It's time to start on demolishing your debts. I think that this is so fraught with emotion it is one of the hardest things to get started, but once you get a taste for it, there will be no stopping you. It's hard to start because initially it can feel soul-destroying when you see money coming in, that you probably feel should be yours, and then feeling like you are giving it all away again. That's why it is so hard to get started, and it is one of the easiest steps to put off. I know that can be how it feels while you are paying your debts down.

It can be hard to remember what it was you spent the money on in the first place, but you **have** to remember because the truth is that you **did spend it**.

I remember when I first secured a contract that paid *really* well. All of a sudden, I had £10,000 per month coming in. Although at the time I had a massive mortgage to go with it, it was still an enormous amount of money. For the first time, I actually had thousands of pounds to spare after my living expenses—and that was every month. The contract was only going to last six months, so I knew I couldn't put things off. The clock was ticking. On my first payday I felt elated. I hadn't been able to imagine that I would ever be capable of earning such a huge amount of money. Now it was a reality, and I was still in shock, but then came the downer. It wasn't mine. I was still in debt. All that money belonged to someone else. You will recall that I was £60,000 in debt. At this point, it was still not much less, so all of my £10,000 cheques for the entire period of the contract were signed away even before it came in. But I knew that I had to bite the bullet if I wanted to be free.

I cannot begin to describe how hard it was to write a cheque for more than half of that first wage cheque and give it to a credit card company. I wanted that money! Waving it goodbye was a nightmare, because when it came in, it felt like it was mine, but it wasn't.

The previous use of that money was long forgotten that day. And it wasn't the last time I would have to do it. There were still many more big cheques to write. I had already been paying off small amounts for years but that had only stopped the debts from getting any bigger. Those payments hadn't really made much of a dent up to that point. The fact that I only had a contract role and not a permanent one was scary at the time. I was still in fear of repossession if anything went wrong. I knew how quickly the tide could come in and drown me if I diverted my attention. Looking back, that contract was a blessing in disguise. Obviously the money was important, but the temporary nature of it was key to my success. This is why; because I knew that the money was only going to be rolling in for a limited time, I had to prioritise.

So let me ask you this. If you had £10,000 a month coming in, and you thought that it was going to keep coming in for as long as you needed it, would you really be incentivised to pay your debts? Probably not! The most likely scenario would be this: as you could easily afford the repayments, you would be tempted to let the debts just run on and on.

It is that exact scenario that got so many people into trouble in the last recession. One day, the money just stopped coming in. The businesses that individuals owned or worked for ran into trouble. Employers left towns in high cost economies and shipped the jobs to China. It happened on a massive scale, and it is still happening today. It will keep happening. It's happening to real people in real households every day of the week. Every single job, no matter how permanent it may appear to be, is only there for as long as it is there. There is no such thing as permanent anymore. You might as well get used to it.

So I had to get down to writing those cheques. I had to go through the pain every month. If you have a sudden flush of money, big or small, imagine that you are on a short term contract and use all the money you can to pay down your debts. When you have got rid of your debts, there will be plenty of time and opportunities to really treat yourself. If an illness or job loss rocks your world, you will be far more stable. You will be more "robust in the face of uncertainty".

So in a moment I am going to share with you a debt reduction system that is simple and that works. Just before I do that, just remind yourself that while you are on the way to your bigger goal of being debt free, you need to keep up all the repayments that you have logged in your weekly or monthly budget. It is assumed that you are doing this while you are creating and following your personal plan to slash and burn those debts.

So let's look at your options for how you go about paying off debts. First of all, I am going to assume that you have more than one debt, and that those debts are spread across various different lenders. The figures in both the UK and the United States say that the average household has more than one debt, so this is a normal debt picture.

Some financial experts suggest paying off the debt with the highest interest rate first, irrespective of size because, technically, that is the most financially efficient way to get rid of debt. However, in my opinion, it's not always the right way. Other experts advocate paying the smallest debt first, so that you get the benefit of seeing yourself making faster progress to dealing with the problem. Personally, I advocate a combination of the two, with some extra thought put into your emotional well-being. This combined approach helps you to keep on track because it also allows you to feel better while your debts are reducing, however slow your progress may be, and yet you are still being fairly financially efficient. By taking the emotional impact of the debt into account up front, it is easier to maintain energy and focus, allows you to build up momentum and gives you a feel-good factor that keeps growing as you work your way through your personal slash and burn plan.

Your aim is to create a plan that suits your personality, conserves or improves your emotional well-being and that gets the job done.

You already have your basic debt repayments built into your budget. You know already that minimum payments are like a life sentence and that I recommended fixed amount repayments. What you are going to do now is to go way beyond even that, so that you can break free from the shackles of your lenders as quickly as possible. Here you are going to go further than fixed payment amounts—much further.

So, let's get going. Step one is this. Uncover any debts that make you feel particularly bad—because you are going to get rid of those first. Simply make a list of everyone that you owe money to. Your list of your debts doesn't even need to show the size of the debts at this stage. All you want to bring to the fore are any particular debts that stress you out above all others. For some people it is the car payment because they know that if car gets repossessed, they can't get to work or get the kids to school. Incidentally, you will find out in another chapter how wealthy people deal with car payments, but for now I suggest you keep the car payment debt high up on the list of debts to get rid of. Just make a note, the debt that really stresses you out the most needs to get crushed first.

Large or small, if it preys on your mind more than the others, you need to get rid of it. You need it gone. That will help you to focus your energy on the big stuff later. Don't even look at the rest of your list for the time being. Put the list in the drawer and forget about it. You can't deal with everything at once, and worrying doesn't pay the debts. Leave the other items until you have paid your "stress" debts off first. Obviously, you keep going with your fixed payments on the rest of the list. You are just going to keep those chunking down (or at the very least, not letting them get any bigger), while you deal with the "stress" debt.

Attack that debt like you have never attacked anything before. Pay off every penny you have spare, and I mean every penny, not just every spare tenner—EVERY PENNY—until the debt is gone. You might need to sell some possessions on eBay. You might have to find a part time job, and you might have to take in some ironing. Who cares? You just have to find a way to get money. You are going to be debt free. If you are ironing for money, every shirt gets you closer to that freedom, remember that.

The process could take weeks, months or years. However long it takes, it's got to be done. The debt won't go away. They never do. If you think no one cares about you, try missing a couple of debt payments! So you have to bite the bullet. Just get your head down, and get it done.

When your first debt is gone, it would be perfectly reasonable to give yourself a small reward. If you don't, you could run out of steam. Plan for a break, and give yourself a date to get started again. Maybe take a week off and put all your spare money into your "spending money" envelope. It's only a short holiday, but it may well be enough to boost your energy before the next big push. Then you can get started again.

After you have paid off the debt that stresses you most, you can start to pay down the rest. Get the list back out of the drawer. Now it's time to start step two, and get a bit more scientific about things. Now it is time to major on the most efficient way to chip away at your debts. Time is money with debt. The longer you take, the more it costs.

So now is the time to look at the *cost* of your debts as well as the size of them.

To perform step two is easy. Just look at your list of all the debt's that are left. At this point, exclude your mortgage. In most households, the mortgage is the biggest debt of all. It is a topic in its own right and should be put to one side for the time being while you get the rest of your finances in good shape. Paying down your mortgage is a great idea, but in this context I consider it more of a wealth building exercise, which is beyond the scope of this book. If that is a goal you have already, great! You can use the same strategies as for other debt pay down, there just might be some extra considerations to take into account. Talk to your mortgage company or your financial advisor for guidance on this. Anyway, for the time being we are going to focus on other debts.

So now you have a list of all the debts that you have left outstanding. This list should by now, have a lot less emotion attached to it. List the debtor, what the debt is for and the interest rate. You need the APR, the annual percentage rate.

Your list will probably end up looking something like this:

Car Loan	Acme Bank	£6,700	12.5%
Credit Card 1	Any Card	£8,000	26.2%
Credit Card 2	Bad Card Ltd	£4,000	18.8%

At this point, you are not looking at the monthly cost of the debt.

If you have lost track of the size of any of the debts, you need to find out by asking your lender or by digging out your last statement of account.

Order the debts with the biggest debt at the top of the list and the smallest at the bottom. If you can't see the APR easily, call your lender and find out the current rate that they are charging you.

Make sure you set up standing orders for the fixed payment amounts. Late payment fees can really do damage to the cost of your debt, and the lenders can put up your interest rate on the debt that if you pay late, because you become a higher risk to them. Avoid late payment at all costs.

Generally, I suggest you pay off the smallest debts first unless you see that you have a debt with a truly horrific interest rate. If that's the case, make it a priority. We will come back to that in a moment. Paying the smallest debt off in its entirety first makes you feel better, and you will increase in confidence as a person as you go along. You will also free up another chunk of your repayment budget to roll across to a different debt. Because each time you clear a debt altogether, you free up another lump of money, which used to go to that lender, to divert to the next debt. This is the start of compound interest working **for you**, not against you (in a way).

That leaves you with the biggest debt last; but at least ALL your debt repayment budget will then be going to paying off that one debt. Your biggest debt will get paid off faster than you could have done while you were spreading your money across lots of different priorities. You get to put all your fire power into the debt that needs it most.

The only exception I would make is this.

Don't follow the smallest debt strategy if there is a *huge* difference in interest rates, the odd percentage point doesn't count. I am talking about a really big difference in rates here. For example, if you have a bank loan at 10% and a credit card loan at 32% that 22% rate difference *would* warrant temporarily altering the "pay the smallest debt first" strategy. If you have a debt like this, either pay it off first (so it reduces the speed at which debt piles on interest), or do a balance transfer of that high interest debt to another lender who will give you a lower rate. Balance transfers are fine as long as you don't use them just to avoid paying the debt for a longer period.

Do not just leave a high rate debt sitting there piling on the compound interest, when you can either pay it off or transfer it to a lender who will offer you a better deal.

Whichever debts you end up paying first, just keep putting all your energy into one debt at a time and watch each one reduce until it's gone. Like you did with the emotional "stress debt", simply pay off every penny you can. Have the strength of character to admit to as many people as you can that you are paying down debt at the moment. It will help you in social situations, and it will mean that you are no longer keeping secrets. You don't have to broadcast it—just don't allow social pressure to get you to behave in ways that aren't in line with what you can really afford.

People will understand that you are doing a good thing. If they are in debt themselves but they are still in denial about it, they will be secretly admiring you and wishing they had your courage. It probably won't be long before they will be coming to you for advice about doing the same thing. Tell them where they can buy this book! You have nothing to be ashamed of while you are living within your means. In fact, it's clear to you now that you need to live well below the level of your previous lifestyle while you are paying debts off. You can be proud of yourself.

Just remember that by doing this now, you are releasing yourself from the bondage of working for someone else for the rest of your life. Stop working for the banks and the finance companies, and instead start to work for your **own** future. The finance companies may not care about you, but you certainly should!.

Doing all this may be simple, but it is a brave set of steps to take. Just know deep inside that you are right. You know that it is the ONLY step to take. It may feel more like a leap than a step to you right now, but you have to trust yourself and do it anyway. You have so much to be proud of for taking it. You **are** worth it.

You can keep up with all of these steps until you have your rainy day fund always intact, you are free of consumer debt, you own your car (more about that shortly) and all you have left owing is your mortgage. Oh yes, and the fact is that by then, most of what you earn now is yours to keep. You can start to enjoy your own money (about time!) and think about saving and investing for the future. It's an exciting moment when you become free for the first time. Trust me; it is worth working for. I have experienced it, and I experience the joy that it brings every single day. The pleasure of financial freedom really is a daily thrill.

I realise that I am lucky to have had the fortitude to see it through. I even own my house outright. More than one actually, for investment purposes, of course. I didn't buy additional property with fancy no-money-down strategies. I did it by putting **all** the money down. As you know, I like to buy things for cash. If you keep up with good habits, you can have that too.

But before we leave the subject of debt for good, in the final couple of chapters I want to warn you about a few things. I urge you to gain sufficient knowledge to protect yourself throughout your journey from debt and into wealth. So now, before we get finished up let's take a quick look at a few traps that you need to avoid along the way. You need to make sure you don't swim with the sharks.

The Tyranny of Payday Lending and Loan Sharks

"I like my players to be married and in debt.
That's the way you motivate them."
—Ernie Banks, baseball player and coach

I f you have read this far, then you already know the importance of getting yourself in the black, but sometimes people turn to "alternative" forms of borrowing to get themselves out of a scrape. This book wouldn't be complete without a word of warning about the tyranny of such lending and about the so called business practices that abound. These alternative lenders pray on the needy and unfortunate, and specifically encourage the feckless to continue along a path of reality avoidance and self-gratification. The saddest thing of all is that some genuinely needy people end up resorting to them for various reasons without understanding the true costs. That's why it is so important to have a financial education, however basic that may be.

In essence, I implore you to shun using payday lending to help your cash flow with the same level of vigour as you would avoid walking in front of a bus. In fact, these two actions have a lot in common. This grubby business sector, which markets itself as easy access to money for everyone, is a cause of great concern even for the government. A recent investigation by the Office of Fair Trading in the UK has placed sanctions on the **top 50** of them. That's right, they are almost all under investigation. It's a nasty business and our normally meek and mild regulator has announced publicly that many of these companies do business right on the edge of legality. In other words, they are the worst kind of (semi) legal lenders. The UK regulator has recently threatened to close many of these businesses down if they don't comply. They were recently given just 12 weeks to clean up their act—or be shut down.

These companies **do not** have YOUR best interests at heart. They will NOT solve your problems. They exist for people who can't manage their money, and they charge exorbitant interest rates for allowing people to stay in denial about their spending. Even a quick look online showed interest rates are commonly between 4,000% and a staggering 16 MILLION percent.

That's right—you did read it right the first time. 16 MILLION PERCENT Annual Percentage Rate. You don't need to be a mathematician to work out that you should not get involved with such ludicrous rates. Don't be tempted to use debt to solve your debt problems, and NEVER use payday lenders. Eat dry bread, go cleaning, busk with a tin can on the street. Do anything legal to bring in some money. At least you will be working for yourself. Just don't ever go to work for them. They will keep cracking the whip long after they get the principal of the loan back, and they will be cracking for longer than you want to think about—and in ways you don't want to think about.

And just before I get off the subject of high interest lending, never *ever* use loan sharks. They are illegal, they are immoral and you will probably never pay off the debt. The debts are designed for you not to ever get clear of them. Enough said. Time to move on. Let's look at your car costs.

Crushed by Car Costs

"Drive-in banks were established so most of the
cars today could see their real owners."
— E. Joseph Cossman

D o you know how much your car costs you?

We almost all need a car to get around. Unless you live in a big
city with great transport links on your doorstep, you need a car.
But do you know what your car *really* costs?

Did you know that very few wealthy people drive really expensive new
cars? I am talking about your average wealthy family here, and for the context of this chapter, I define that as someone with a million or so of net
worth. More often than not, brand new expensive cars are actually owned
by the bank that lent the money to buy them. Only the super-rich can afford
super-expensive cars. Now, don't get me wrong, I'm not against nice cars.
What I am against is people who can't afford them driving them and losing
lots of money on them. You don't have to drive a super car to burn a lot of
cash. You see very few financially savvy people who have worked hard for
their money choose to drive expensive new cars. As cars have traditionally
been perceived as such a status symbol, that might surprise you.

The reasons that really savvy people tend to do what they do are these. First of all, they have nothing to prove, and the secondly, they understand just how much money new cars *really* cost.

A new car loses between 25% and 40% of its value in the first year, and an average middle of the road brand of car can lose 60% of its value in the first three years. It's called depreciation, and the level of it is truly staggering.

You must have money to burn if you buy a brand new car. Some people change their cars every two years. It's madness! You can save a fortune buying a slightly older car. That's what wealthy people do. While you are still on the road to financial freedom, car payment money can be diverted to paying off other debts, then it can go towards paying off your mortgage (or saving for a deposit if you don't own a property yet). Let's see how, but before I do that, I want you to know that I lead by example here. I will never have a car payment again. I haven't had one in over ten years, and I have a very nice car indeed sitting on my drive.

If you want to be the same, then you need to **do** the same.

I only recently discovered that many other wealthy people do exactly the same as I do, and for the same reasons. What I do is simple. I buy a used car, about one to one and half years old, with dealer mileage on the clock. I look for a car with 6,000 to 15,000 miles on the clock, and when I find the one I like, I pay for it in cash. I get an almost new car for about 60% of the new price, and the depreciation after that is much less.

The reason this is such a sensible strategy is, in part, because of the way car sales are calculated by both car manufacturers and dealers. Both of them want sales numbers to look as good as possible at the end of each quarter, and at the end of each year. They know that they need to stay up in the car sales charts because the motoring press and the newspapers watch sales like hawks. To keep numbers up, unsold cars often get registered and "sold" at the end of each financial quarter. Who do they sell them to? That's easy, surplus stock gets sold internally within the trade. Either a dealer buys them with payment delayed or the manufacturer buys them as "staff cars". The staff get the perk of a nice new car for a few months—and the manufacturer gets the "sale". The cars are kept fully serviced and in mint condition, then they get drip fed into the second hand market, usually through the premier dealerships where they are sold on as "demonstrators".

They are the perfect answer for their price-conscious wealthy buyers that want quality but don't want to stomach the depreciation. The discounts are massive. The dealers would rather sell you a new car on finance of course (it's another way to make money), but they would rather sell you something than let someone else sell you something! They will keep you in the showroom at all costs.

I am not suggesting that you are in a position to buy a nearly-new swanky car for cash yet. But I am suggesting that you do buy whatever you can afford to drive for cash. It is only a temporary measure! If all you can afford is an old banger, drive an old banger. You see, we have been trained as consumers to buy cars based on what we can afford to pay *each month*.

Car dealers can accommodate almost any monthly budget, and they will work really hard to find a way to spend your monthly budget for you. They can play with the interest rate, the length of the repayment period and even some discounting. They will do everything in their power to get you locked in for years. Their job isn't to look after your finances; their job is to sell you a car.

It's **your job** to look after your finances, and to do that you need to buy your car for cash. Get out of those car payments as quickly as you can. I suggest to you that you should sell your precious car if you can't afford to buy out your finance today. If you have a car payment, you are in debt; and being shackled by debt is your biggest barrier to becoming financially liberated. It is the mental angle as well. If you only drive what you can afford, you are being true to yourself, and you aren't pretending to people that you are something that you're not.

Most people take huge loans out for cars. They are the biggest single payment many people have after their rent or mortgage. Did you know that General Motors has over 11 BILLION dollars out in lending to consumers, mostly for the cars they manufacture? That is one heck of a lot of people with car payments!

Do you really need the car you are driving now as badly as you need to unload the burden of the payment that goes with it? Until you are financially free, probably not. The wise course of action is to downgrade the car as much as you can. The plan is to buy as reliable a car as you can for cash, and keep it until either it falls apart, or you can afford a better one. That's until you are financially free of course; then you can do what you like.

You can have three new Aston Martin's then, if that is what floats your boat. In the meantime, just remember that most wealthy people use the strategy of buying a not quite new, decent quality car, looking after it and driving it for years. They don't need to show off their wealth. They know that many of the better/newer/bigger cars on the road aren't even owned by the driver, they are owned by the finance company. I can tell you that it's a good feeling.

So save up your cash until you can buy an old banger for cash and drive it until you can afford a better, newer banger. Bit by bit you can work your way back. Sure, you might lose a little money on the trade once or twice, but losing 40% of a small amount of money isn't very much of a loss. You are aiming to buy a car for about three months' worth of car payments or as close to that as you can.

When you haven't got those car payments draining you each month, you will be amazed at how quickly you start to accumulate money. Some of it can go towards buying another car later on. I do understand that an older car may be a bit less reliable, so put away the next two payments you would have made toward a car repair fund. You have your rainy day fund as well, so you should be prepared for any little surprises. You don't need to be too fearful about breakdowns though; cars are much more reliable than they were even ten years ago. An older car won't let you down as much as you might imagine. How many breakdowns do you see on the roads these days?

I remember how hard it was when my BMW almost got repossessed. I was so down at the time, and so broke, that the car seemed to represent my last shred of pride. I was still clinging to the illusion that everything would be fine, that my next big idea would work and my fortune was just around the next corner. It wasn't, and until I had the courage to admit my real situation and get rid of the car and the payments, I wasn't able to get out of denial or out of debt.

I swapped my stunning navy blue BMW for an old banger. I bought a ten-year-old Vauxhall that leaked. Even though I took a financial hit on the value of the car, my outgoings reduced by almost £500 a month overnight. I was in sales then, and I had to park around the corner so my clients couldn't see my car. It was a hard thing to do but a good thing to do. I couldn't believe the feeling of freedom that I had when I finally let go of the self-delusion and dumped the car.

So if you are struggling financially and you have a nice car on the never-never, stop cheating yourself and downgrade it.

You will be able to upgrade again when you can afford it. It's the only sensible thing to do. So enough of the talk of going down in status temporarily and bringing some sense back to your car costs, let's look at the good part. Let's look at accumulating money, how it works and why you will feel better when you do it.

Start a Savings Habit and Take the Upper Hand

"A penny here, and a dollar there, placed at interest, goes on accumulating, and in this way the desired result is attained. It requires some training, perhaps, to accomplish this economy, but when once used to it, you will find there is more satisfaction in rational saving than in irrational spending."
—P. T. Barnum

So, you want to be an investor? An investor is someone who has learned ways to make their money work for them, so they don't need to work as hard in a job or a business. But before you can become an investor, you need some seed capital.

Once you have worked hard and are rid of your debts, the money you used to use to make repayments can go into creating a foundation for your future wealth. Sure you will have to start small, but as you already know, starting small allows you to find your feet.

This next part is really simple.

Making money from money is possible. Remember the terrifying cost of debt—that it was a thing called "compound interest" that saddles people for years in debt that can be almost impossible to clear on minimum payments?

Well, when you have money—instead of owing money—compound interest works the other way round, too. You EARN interest on interest, instead of paying it. You probably recall that Einstein called it the eighth wonder of the world.

Getting started as an investor just takes some self-discipline. You simply need to allocate money as carefully to long term savings in the same way you allocated money to debt repayments. If you spend all the money you previously spent on repaying debts on having a good time, you will never be wealthy. You have to *learn* to save.

Wealthy women don't do what most other people do. Most people do this: they spend what they have to, then save what's left. The trouble is there never is any left! But you don't do that anymore, do you...

Wealthy women do it the other way round. They make a budget, stick to it and find out how much they can save as soon as their pay cheque arrives. They SAVE FIRST, and SPEND WHAT'S LEFT.

So start saving TODAY.

Now you are debt free, you can allow yourself some treats. Before you splash out too much, I would advise you to make sure that you have at least six months' money in the bank so if you have a real disaster you won't fall back into debt again. When I was contracting, I always knew that there was the capacity to run out of money if the contract stopped suddenly, and contracts nearly always stop suddenly—companies take on contractors because they can get rid of them quickly, that is why the pay is higher. It did teach me to look after my money better. It taught me I had to plan ahead. Knowing I had a few months' money tucked away in the bank allowed me to be more relaxed. I didn't relax my financial budgeting skills, but I did relax myself as a person.

If you have kept your lifestyle simple, it might take a little while to do that but trust the fact that it is well worth it. Start with getting one week ahead, then one month ahead, and build up from there. You don't have to be an investor to feel secure. Knowing that you have some money set aside will give you an incredible feeling of security long before you become truly wealthy.

Start putting the money that you were using for debt payments into a simple savings account to start with. Then search around for a tax-efficient easy-access place to put your savings. Investment is really outside the scope of this book. But once you have developed a saving habit, it won't be long before your financial confidence starts to grow.

Don't Get Shafted

"I know a baseball star who wouldn't report the theft of his wife's credit cards because the thief spends less than she does."
—Joe Garagiola

This seems like a prudent moment to mention how easily, once you start building your nest egg, it can be taken away from you. Scams are rife, and they come in many different forms.

Anyone who says that money is complicated stuff is either not very good with it themselves, or could be trying to justify taking some of yours. Perpetuating the idea that making money is a highly technical affair, and complicating it with technical jargon and unfathomable rules, regulations and variables, is an easy way to get people who lack financial confidence to hand their money over. Remember that while financial advisors are qualified to understand the rules, they aren't necessarily good with money themselves. I have known of several who can barely keep their own head above water, yet spend their day telling other people how to make money. Most bank managers are there to bring the bank profits by lending out money to customers and selling them financial products. They are not there to make you wealthy. Very few bank managers are wealthy, the wages are modest and precious few of them understand anything at all about investing money. In other words, be very careful who you choose to advise you.

As soon as you have some money, people and companies will come at you from every direction trying to get their hands on some of it. You will have financial services products being thrown at you from every direction. Stick with simple, easy to understand products and go to the best buy guides on reputable financial websites that can be trusted to provide good legal information. They aren't too hard to find. You really need a wealthy person to guide you and warn you about the latest fads. Read the papers (just remember that there aren't so many wealthy journalists either so there is a limit to what they know too), keep yourself informed. If you don't have any wealthy friends, you need to start knowing where they hang out. Get prepared for being wealthy yourself.

Let's just take a moment to look at scams. There are many that are specifically targeted at women. Online dating and friendships are pots of gold for the scammers, and they frequently target women who are looking for love. The police don't have numbers of exactly how much fraud is conducted online these days; most people are so embarrassed that they don't report it. Sadly, only the most desperate cases come to their attention.

Take the sad case of Brenda Parkes. She was 60 years old when she was scammed out of £60,000 by an online fraudster. She went public with it to prevent other people being taken in by such scams. She said that she perceived herself as a professional intelligent woman and couldn't believe how she had been taken in bit by bit. She knows it's very unlikely she will ever get her money back. Years of prudent financial planning and caring attention was wiped out by one wicked person over a very short period of time. Be on your guard.

Scammers don't just target naive people either. Competent professional women get scammed too, and relationship scams are just the tip of the iceberg. Investment scams are rife, too. Promises of big returns are all too common, and if it looks too good to be true, it usually is. Even Nicola Horlick, the so-called super woman, got caught. Nicola ran a high-profile investment company and got caught up in the Bernie Madoff Ponzi scheme. She lost millions of her clients' money.

There will also be sob stories from family members and others who think that because you have a little bit put aside you can help them too, and it can be very tempting. Very few of us like saying no to children or loved ones, so if you can afford to give them money, it's your money to give, go right ahead.

Lending money is a different matter. It is better to give than to lend. If you lend to people close to you, it is unlikely that you will get the money back. If you are lucky enough to have your money returned, there is the risk that damage to the relationship will be done because of the stress and obligation placed on both parties. In the long term, you probably won't help as much as you would like anyway, because you know that each of us must learn our own worth and learn how to manage our emotions and our own money.

Fortify Your Credit History

"Save a part of your income and begin now, for the man with a surplus controls circumstances and the man without a surplus is controlled by circumstances."
—Henry Buckley

Although you might still be trying to get rid of your debts, if you want a mortgage at any point, it is important that you look after your credit history.

Owning your own property, even if the bank helps you to do it, is a good idea on many levels. That's assuming you buy the right property, do your research, have a backup plan in place and it goes without saying (but I will say it anyway) that you can afford the repayments. To be able to do that, you will probably need to borrow money, so you do need to look after your credit history. Any mortgage company will want to know that you will pay back your loan.

Before we go further and explore the ins and outs of credit history, I feel it is appropriate to talk briefly about property as an investment. It is relevant here because we are talking about your credit history in the context of potentially getting a mortgage in the future if you don't already have one, or ever plan to get another one.

Many people have made money out of property over the years. In the last recession and associated property crash, many people lost money, and a large number lost their homes altogether. Detailed information about property is out of the scope of this book, but there are some general thoughts that I feel compelled to insert at this point. If you are looking to buy a home, 'home' is the important word. A home is not an investment. It is a home. In fact, it is a liability because it costs money to service it and pays you zero return on your money while you are living in it. A house is only an investment when someone else is paying YOU to live in it. One last thing about property is that if you use any increase in property values as some sort of brick built ATM, then you become highly vulnerable in the event of a financial storm. Property should be a savings mechanism, not a spending mechanism. Ask all the people that increased the size of their mortgages and spent the money on consumer goods and holidays in the good times how they are feeling now?

I digressed deliberately, but now we can get back on track. You are making your own credit history every week that goes by. Even if you don't think of it that way, trust me when I tell you that your bank and credit card company does. When you take on a commitment to pay something, you are making a promise—a promise to use someone else's money, property, time or service in return for a payment. Credit is simply a promise to pay for something AFTER you have started to have the benefit from it.

How good you are to your word is called your "credit history".

The credit reference agencies that lenders use get paid to record your habits of keeping your promises. They help companies and financial institutions to assess the likelihood that you, as a borrower, will stick to your side of the contract. You need to do everything in your power to honour your promises to them. If you don't, you will end up paying dearly.

Credit reference agencies keep huge amounts of data, and some of it can be wrong. Take action to make sure the records are up to date. You do not need to take a paid service; you can check your credit history for free. Take your credit record seriously as it will determine not only your ability to buy your own home but the interest rate that you will pay.

So look after your credit history. There is plenty of help online that you can find to help you re-build a poor credit history. It's not the end of the world, it just takes some work.

So enough about budgeting, cars, spending, avoiding the biggest pitfalls and starting to build some savings. Let's wrap up by talking about the most exciting step of all. You are now ready to start learning how to make your money work harder than you do.

That is called investing.

Slavery to Mastery

"Speculation is an effort, probably unsuccessful, to turn a little money into a lot. Investment is an effort, which should be successful, to prevent a lot of money from becoming a little."
—Fred Schwed, Jr.

Moving from debt to wealth is a long, sometimes arduous journey, but one that is well worth the effort involved. The whole trip can be outrageously exciting and stimulating too; it's not all about hard work! It's also about having fun, learning lots of fascinating stuff and meeting some amazing people.

Here is a fascinating fact. If you or someone in your family had bought a single share in the Coca-Cola Company in 1919 for $40, that single share (with dividends re-invested) would have been worth a staggering $9.8 million by 2012.[7] OK, back then, $40 was a fair amount of money, somewhere slightly north of $500 today (approx. £350 in UK sterling). That is still only a few nights out and less than most people's car repayment.

This share example illustrates beautifully the power that relatively modest amounts of money invested over a long period of time can have. If you want to find out more about the Coke story, and the details of how the amount was calculated, just Google it. By the way, if you haven't come across dividends as a term yet, here is what they are. When you own a "share", you literally own a piece of that company, so you also own part of the profits. The proportion of the company profits that is paid to your "share" is called a "dividend".

To become wealthy it will, at some point, be time to move on from just earning money. You will move to the concept of making money. It is different even from investing. Earning money involves taking money from other people in return for your time. Essentially, earning involves transfer of wealth from one pocket to another. The concept of making money is different. That is where you create something that wasn't there before and put a value on it. When you create something totally new and unique, you start to make your own market.

Although the practicalities of earning increasing amounts of money and going on to invest it are outside the scope of this book, it is a good time to share with you some of the joys that it brings. Knowing that there is joy beyond paying off debt and creating stability is important because we all need to look beyond our current situation.

This book has mainly been about learning to direct your mind, shake off things that had previously held you back and giving you some practical skills to get yourself onto an even keel.

I would have loved to have had the space to include a guide on the process of actually making the money as well; but sadly there wasn't the space to do it here, and it would have diluted the message of possibility and responsibility that is the greatest freedom of all. There was a danger that the shiny money-making parts of a larger book would have excited your inner elephant in the wrong way and allowed you to be dragged back into the traditional fairytale. The one that goes along the lines of "when you have more money, all your problems disappear".

You now know that it's not true that money solves everything. There are problems it can solve and problems it can't. Your happiness can be independent of your financial situation up to a point. Happiness is a decision, not something that happens *to you* when you have money.

You know that the real rewards of your self-discipline, perseverance and achievements are much bigger than money, and that the money is an outcome. As one of my mentors likes to say, the money is the silent applause for a job well done. The money is something that you can look forward to if you keep on the road for long enough.

The joy of investing, of turning money into a crop that produces more of itself over time, is a worthy goal. You can also do a lot of good with your investments. None of us can work forever, but it is also up to each of us to pay our way throughout our lives, not just until we run out of energy, inclination or ability. We should all be able to stop worrying about ever running out.

There is some fear about investing, and that's a good thing. It is rare that you can invest without any fear—it keeps you on your toes. Money is all about sentiment, not about sentimentality; but you already know that.

When I invest, I don't look for above average returns because I don't want to take above average risk. There is a unique risk/reward profile for everyone. When it's your turn to invest (which is when you have enough savings that you don't need to worry about breaking into it all the time to escape from emergencies) you will have some work to do. You will need to establish what you need your money to do for you and how much risk you are prepared to take to get it to work at the right intensity.

Just remember this about investing: an investment is only an investment if you allow it to grow. Your seed capital is just that—seed. Your seeds can only become a field full of dreams if you don't eat the first crop!

If you are tempted to eat the fruits of your seed capital, you are not building a long term financial future for yourself; you are just deferring your spending. You really must allow your money to grow. You need to walk away from it for a while. Like a crop, it won't grow any faster if you sit there watching over it. You are better to use your time to work hard and increase the amount of seed that you have. Just one further note on early investments: make sure any investments you have at the beginning are low risk and tax efficient.

It's your job to create your money, look after it, enjoy yourself along the way, live with passion and invest in your own growth. If you do that, you will be able to look forward to a life of security and harmony. It all starts between your ears and ends between your ears.

The game of wealth is worth every minute, every micron of your attention so that you can escape the shackles forever. It is worth it, so that you can live the life that you design for yourself.

You bring home the bacon at the beginning, and then as time goes by, you can start to let the bacon look after you.

I leave you with this wish—that you enjoy the trip as much as I have so far.

I hope that one day soon, you will be able to step up and know that there is nothing that can come into view that you cannot cope with, one way or another. Then, when you look out to the sea of possibilities, this is your future: it will be across a vision of golden sands with a cool cocktail in your hand. Jamaica in February is great! Maybe we will meet there one day? If we do, I will know that you have escaped the shackles, stepped up to a richer life and that you can enjoy every bacon sandwich that your heart desires—and more.

Endnotes

1. If you are interested in 'confirmation bias' research, read *Decisive* by Chip and Dan Health
2. Simon Sinek - *Start With Why, How Great Leaders Inspire Everyone to Take Action.* Published by Penguin
3. The Rules Of Wealth, Richard Templar, Penguin Education Limited, Second Edition © Richard Templar and Pearson Education Ltd 2012
4. source: Moneysavingexpert.com - credit card calculator
5. Moneysavingexpert.com - credit card calculator
6. Long Term Capital Management (LTCM) almost collapsed in 1998 despite being based on financial models created by 2 Nobel Prize winning economists
7. http://www.dailyfinance.com/2012/08/14/ coca-cola-stock-share-worth-millions/

For more information about
Sophie and her books, visit:

www.sophiebennettauthor.com

Lightning Source UK Ltd.
Milton Keynes UK
UKOW04f1415010514

230938UK00001B/7/P